BACKFIRE

A Collection of Short Stories from the
Caribbean for use in Secondary Schools

Compiled by

Neville and Undine Giuseppi

MACMILLAN
CARIBBEAN

Macmillan Education
Between Towns Road, Oxford OX4 3PP
A division of Macmillan Publishers Limited
Companies and representatives throughout the world

www.macmillan-caribbean.com

ISBN 0 333 15219 0

First published 1973

Printed in Thailand

2009 2008 2007 2006 2005 2004
41 40 39 38 37 36 35 34 33 32

Contents

Page

Acknowledgments iv
Introduction v

Backfire   Shirley Tappin   1
Paradise Lost   Ida Ramesar   7
Chung Lee   Undine Giuseppi   14
Give and Take   Robert Henry   20
The Kite   Barnabas J. Ramon-Fortuné   24
Horace's Luck   Neville Giuseppi   34
Mama's Theme Song   Joy Moore   38
The Teddy Bear   C. Arnold Thomasos   46
De Trip   Joy Clarke   52
The Hustlers   Flora Spencer   58
Journey by Night   Undine Giuseppi   64
The New Teacher   Ninnie Seereeram   68
Up the Wind
     Laka Notoo-Boy   Ian Robertson   73
After the Game   Barnabas J. Ramon-Fortuné   78
Ramgoat Salvation   Ida Ramesar   85
Tantie Gertrude   Oliver Flax   92
The Cousins   Joy Moore   98

About the Contributors   111

Acknowledgments

For permission to reprint copyright material the publishers and the compilers are grateful to Barnabas J. Ramon-Fortuné for 'The Kite'; Robert Henry for 'Give and Take'; Ida Ramesar for 'Paradise Lost' and 'Ramgoat Salvation'; Ninnie Seereeram for 'The New Teacher'; Flora Spencer for 'The Hustlers'; and Shirley Tappin for 'Backfire'.

We wish also to thank those contributors who wrote stories specially for this collection: Joy Clarke for 'De Trip'; Oliver Flax for 'Tantie Gertrude'; Barnabas J. Ramon-Fortuné for 'After the Game'; Joy Moore for 'The Cousins' and a revised version of 'Mama's Theme Song'; Ian Robertson for 'Up the Wind Laka Notoo-Boy'; and C. Arnold Thomasos for 'The Teddy Bear'.

Our thanks are due also to Joy Ackbarali, who prepared the sections entitled 'Time for Talking and Writing', and expressed certain views which have been incorporated in the Introduction.

Introduction

This collection of stories embraces the work of two generations of West Indian writers–the old and the new. Barnabas J. Ramon-Fortuné, Neville Giuseppi, Undine Giuseppi, Flora Spencer and C. Arnold Thomasos have all been writing and publishing from as far back at least as the 1930's and 1940's. With the exception of Robert Henry, whose story 'Give and Take' appeared in *Focus,* a Jamaican publication, in 1960, all the other young writers are new to the West Indian literary scene. Ida Ramesar, though not a West Indian by birth, has identified herself with the West Indies, and on this basis she has earned for herself a place in this collection.

Though the writers are drawn from different generations, the stories which they have written reflect no recognisable differences which might be attributed to that fact. 'De Trip' by Joy Clarke is a story written entirely in dialect, but it will appeal to most West Indians, who will recognise it as being true to life.

The book is intended for use in the Junior Secondary School, the particular year being dependent on the level of maturity of the pupils. This often varies from school to school, but the Second and Third Formers are the ones for whom it will most likely be found suitable.

Backfire is meant to set the imagination of both the teacher and the student afire. We hope that it will challenge the teacher to deepen and expand the vision and expression of his students.

Our children have much to say about their own world, but often they cannot translate what they feel into meaningful language. The stories selected and the sections called 'Time for Talking and Writing' are intended specifically to stir the feelings and evoke some response from the children, for the stories are all about children and people

INTRODUCTION (cont'd)

very much like themselves. It is hoped that students will want to talk about some of the situations depicted, and be inspired to comment on their own society. Talking is really the first step to formulating ideas. We hope that as teachers help students to discover meaning from the stories, careful attention will be given to the way in which the students express and formulate their ideas.

The questions set out in 'Time for Talking and Writing' are designed to give scope not only for picking out the obvious but also for putting together more than one idea to form an impression and thus express an opinion. In several instances there are suggestions for paragraph writing on specific subjects. We hope these will be suitable exercises for helping students to state logically and convincingly their ideas. There are also some exercises that can provide opportunities for imaginative writing.

Subjects of a controversial nature arising out of some of the stories should be used for class discussion or debate. The teacher should make use of current issues that are relevant to the discussion. In that way relevance will become a reality in our schools. Students are never too young to learn to comment logically on their environment.

Reading aloud these stories in class should 'be done regularly, for there is much to enjoy publicly as well as privately. Often stories, well-read, can have a strong impact which leaves a lasting impression. We hope that using *Backfire* will be a pleasurable literary experience for both teacher and student. There is no limit to what an enthusiastic person can do with these stories.

Neville and Undine Giuseppi

Backfire

It was a hot, sunny day in Port-of-Spain.

People were hustling up and down Frederick Street anxious, it seemed, to reduce the contents of the pay packets they had received a day or two before, for it was the end of the month.

The limers were in their usual places – at the corners and in front of the stores – observing the hustle and bustle, digging the chicks, heckling and ole-talking.

Beulah Sampson counted out ninety-four dollars and fifty cents, put it into her handbag and hurried out of the Bank into upper Frederick Street.

Ever since her husband Albert, or 'Bertie' as she preferred to call him, had got into that automobile accident three years ago, she came every month into Port-of-Spain to draw his pension.

It was on one of these occasions that Beulah's now deep-rooted habit had begun. She could remember the day Bertie found out what she had been up to on her trips into Port-of-Spain – how he had raved and fretted.

'Oh Gord, woman, what wrong wid yuh? Yuh goin' mad or something? I ent able wid no police comin' in me house and searching up, nuh? Yuh better stop yuh damn stupidness. If I had me two foot I wouldn'ta mind so much. Yuh deserve whatever yuh get, but when yuh sit down dey in de jail who go attend to me? I car do nuttin for myself.'

'Oh, shut up, Bertie. What yuh gettin' on so for? Ent I does go and get yuh pension for yuh and bring back every cent? Yuh know where every las' cent does go. By de time I go and buy food and pay rent and ting de money done. Whatever else I do is me damn business. Yuh don't have to meddle in it.'

'Beulah, listen to me. For Gord sake stop what yuh doin'. If de police don't hold yuh, Gord go punish yuh bad, bad. Dey

1

have plenty people worse off than we and dey does get along.'

It was no use arguing, Beulah thought. He would never understand. Time and again he would fret, especially on the days when she brought home his pension.

But how was he to know the thrill it gave her; the excitement it stirred in her; the feeling of satisfaction and victory she got when it was accomplished—not to mention the material gain?

Of course, it was not like that in the beginning.

Pushing her way down Frederick Street, Beulah remembered that first time. It was a day very much like this day. She had just drawn Bertie's pension and was hurrying to get a taxi to go back home when she suddenly remembered that the following Monday was Bertie's birthday.

Surely, she thought, she could squeeze out a little two dollars and get him a gift to cheer him up a bit on his birthday. Her mind made up, she entered the store she was then about to pass.

The first thing that caught her eye was an array of men's socks. Well, she could forget that. Bertie would never need socks for the rest of his life.

She moved on to the second counter and viewed with interest the variety of knick-knacks displayed. A pen and pencil set? . . . No, that wouldn't do. Besides, it looked too expensive . . . well then, a pipe? Eh, eh. Bertie was a cigarette man. . . .

Then she saw it. Bertie would surely appreciate that. She called to the attendant.

'Miss, how much for dis little cigarette lighter?'

'Six ninety-five.'

'Oh Gord, dese people go kill we,' she thought. 'A little stupidy ting like dat—six ninety-five!'

The attendant was taken up with another customer and Beulah began to move to the next counter when, on a sudden impulse, she turned, picked up the lighter, dropped it into her handbag and hurried towards the door.

Even now, walking down Frederick Street so many months after that first incident, she could still vividly remember the tense moments that followed.

She could barely have kept her knees from buckling under

her as she walked away from the store. Beads of perspiration had formed on her forehead and she could sense a thousand accusing eyes boring into her retreating back. She was expecting to feel at any moment an arresting hand on her shoulder. She had never before wished so desperately to be in a taxi heading for San Juan.

On her way home that day it dawned on her that, after all, it was so very simple. A victorious smile played on her lips. She was sure that she could do it again.

Since then Beulah rarely returned home from her trips into Port-of-Spain without some material evidence of her skill.

Beulah was now approaching Queen Street. She had never tried her hand at the really big department stores, for she believed that the chance of being noticed was less in the smaller, more crowded stores. Nevertheless, she was getting more confident and today made up her mind to take the plunge.

She paused for a moment like an animal stalking its prey. Then she deliberately crossed the street and passed through the wide doors that a little later might seem to her not wide enough. A feeling of apprehension came over her and she felt a chill run down her spine.

She cautiously made her way to the Cosmetics Counter and noted with relief that the store was more crowded than she had anticipated. She pressed herself against the counter and fingered a tin of body powder and some after-shave lotion.

'You want something, Madam?' The salesgirl barely glanced at her.

'Is all right, Miss. I jus' lookin'.'

Beulah moved on a bit, then her deft fingers quickly picked up a bottle of cologne and dropped it into a paper bag which had been skilfully manoeuvred and held open in readiness.

Her action was smooth, neat, and carried the finesse that came with Beulah's kind of experience.

As she turned to leave, she bumped into someone who, she realised with horror, was standing right behind her, and she came face to face with a tall, dark man wearing a pair of dark glasses.

She came face to face with a tall, dark man.

Beulah was petrified. Her impulse was to run for dear life out of the store, but the man blocked her path and she felt her blood suddenly go cold. Was Bertie's prophecy about to come true?

She almost collapsed with relief when the man grumbled: 'Look way yuh goin', nuh, woman.'

Beulah all but ran out of the store and back up Frederick Street. It was only when she was safely on her way home that she began to think what might have happened if the man had turned out to be a store detective, as she had feared.

She could hear Bertie's voice: 'I told yuh so. Sooner or later dey was bound to catch up wid yuh. Lord, what go happen to me now?'

Beulah closed her eyes, glad it was all over. She must remember to be more careful in future. With a start she realised that they had already passed Fernandes. She called out: 'Driver, drop me Tenth Avenue.'

She opened her purse to pay the driver. Suddenly her face was transfixed with a look of utter horror and disbelief. She raised her hand to her gaping mouth and gasped, 'Oh Gord! Somebody teef me wallet!'

In a snackette on Henry Street a man was finishing his second drink.

He was feeling pleased with himself for being ninety-odd dollars richer than he had been an hour ago. Finally, he rose to go.

He was a tall, dark man, and he wore a pair of dark glasses.

SHIRLEY TAPPIN

Time for Talking and Writing

1. What particular time of the month did Beulah come into Port-of-Spain? Why did she make these trips every month?

2. Bertie couldn't leave his home. Why was that so?
3. The first article Beulah stole was . . .
4. Where did Beulah commit her first theft? What made her steal on that occasion?
5. Where did Beulah and Bertie live?
6. Why was Beulah encouraged to continue stealing?
7. Pick out the statements that are *true* and those that are *false*. Then explain why each statement is either true or false. (Use a separate line for each statement.)
    (i) Bertie encouraged Beulah to steal because he needed many things.
    (ii) A detective spotted Beulah stealing the bottle of cologne.
    (iii) Beulah realised her husband's money was missing before she reached home.
    (iv) Her money had dropped out from her purse in the store.
8. What do you think these words and phrases might mean: digging the chicks; ole-talking; apprehension; manoeuvred; finesse; petrified.
9. The story ends with the description of a certain man. Where else in the story has he appeared and in what connection?
10. Beulah wasn't only a thief. She had many other better qualities. Explain how this is so.
11. Can you suggest some of the causes for stealing in your country? What do you think should be done to remove those causes?
12. There is a local expression which you can put in place of the title *Backfire*. Can you say what that expression is?
13. The story ends before Beulah arrives at her home. Invent for yourself the excuse Beulah would give to Bertie for the money that was lost.
14. How do you think the backfire would affect Beulah's stealing habit? What lesson is the writer of this story trying to impress upon us?

Paradise Lost

It would be difficult to say exactly when Jimmy became restless and discontented. Impossible to point at any one incident or event and say that was when it began. Suffice it to say that, from a reasonably contented Trinidadian, he became, over a period of months, a highly discontented human being, thoroughly disgusted with his surroundings, his teaching job, and his way of life.

Little things which formerly he had not noticed now became major grievances. Every time his car hit a pot-hole he cursed the island, her people and her Government. Haphazard garbage collection and his over-crowded classroom all did their part to hasten his decision to offer his brain for draining. Wider horizons beckoned him and far-off pastures became more alluring. What if he had a good job and a house of his own!

The Prophets of Doom were quick to point out how much he would be leaving behind, but friends returning from North America painted a glowing picture of their life-style and the wonderful opportunities offered.

From the thought to the actuality there stretched the long road of form-filling, medicals and sundry bits of red tape, but Jimmy braved the hurdles and emerged triumphant with his Canadian visa.

On a bright morning in September he arrived at Piarco, bound for the promised land, his Mecca, the big country with the big heart. He was leaving his island in the sun with no regrets–just a deep sympathy for those who would remain behind in this God-forsaken place. Piarco, as usual, was jammed full of people. Trinidadians obey an unwritten law wherein it is stated that no son or daughter of the soil shall be allowed to leave the island without an escort of at least twenty well-wishers seeing him or her off. All this, of course, resulting as it inevitably did in complete chaos, was another source of annoyance to Jimmy. Passengers and non-passengers mingled merrily with no regard for signs to the contrary. People entered blithely through doors marked 'EXIT', and left through those marked 'ENTRY'. As far as Jimmy was concerned the whole thing was typical; no organisation at all! By some miracle, planes managed to leave more or less on time, and passengers somehow boarded the correct aircraft.

Seated finally in his Toronto-bound plane, Jimmy breathed a sigh of relief and happily bade farewell to pot-holes and all the other trials and tribulations which had beset his life up to then. The future glowed with bright promise.

Toronto airport bristled with efficiency. Baggage was collected with effortless ease, and Jimmy, practically dizzy with happiness, stood at the Immigration desk.

'May I see your passport and visa, Sir, please.'

The officer was very efficient, and Jimmy fumbled through his briefcase for the precious documents. Very much aware of the waiting line of people, he finally located them.

'Here you are, Sir!'

Unsmilingly the officer scrutinised the papers, then stamped them 'Landed Immigrant', and Jimmy passed through the portals into Paradise.

'Hey, Jimmy, over here, boy.'

Coming through the crowd was Vishnu, grinning broadly, waiting to meet him as promised.

'Is good to see you, boy. I have a taxi waiting.'

Then the drive into the city, huge buildings, neon lights, the whole panorama spread before him! The car finally came to a stop before a very tall building.

'Is called a high rise, boy, twenty floors. We live on the tenth.'

Jimmy stood on the pavement and gazed about. A fountain splashed in the court of the building, illuminated by a floodlight, and trees grew in a semi-circle around the court.

Vishnu watched him with an amused expression on his face. 'We have a swimming pool on the fourth floor, and even a sauna bath.'

Jimmy, suitably impressed, replied, 'Vishnu, this is real high-class living, boy.'

Inside they entered the express elevator, reaching the

The officer scrutinised the papers.

tenth floor about twenty seconds before Jimmy's stomach.

'That thing always travel so fast, boy?'

'You get used to it, man.'

The one-bedroom apartment seemed small, but Vishnu said it was plenty big enough for three of them. Smokey, the other occupant, worked nights, and $155.00 split three ways was a lot easier to meet.

'You brought some rum, boy?'

'Of course, man.'

Vishnu grinned. 'Some of the boys coming over for an ole-talk and drink.'

Just then a noise like a ship in distress filled the apartment causing Jimmy to leap from his chair.

'What happen, what happen?'

Vishnu doubled up with laughter. 'Is only the intercom, man, the boys reach.'

Soon the room was filled with laughing Trinidadians.

'Where you from, man?' Questions were fired at him from all sides as representatives from San Juan, Belmont, San Fernando, Couva, and it seemed every little town and village in Trinidad tried to absorb the news from home.

As the ole-talk and questions went on, Jimmy gradually became aware that the picture now being painted of Canadian life was totally unlike the one painted by the boys on holiday at home.

'Man, this place hard, six months I here and is only Security Guard job I get.' This from a former Civil Servant!

'Wait till you register with 'Manpower' and they give you the old "No Canadian experience" run round.'

Jimmy, feeling very superior, retorted, 'But I have my Degree, man, surely I won't have any trouble.'

There was general laughter all round.

'Boy, nobody told you they have Ph.D.s on welfare here?'

A nagging worry emerged at the back of Jimmy's mind. Supposing he couldn't get a job! No, that was impossible. If he couldn't get a teaching job he could always go into the Civil Service.

On a cold wind-swept Toronto street a lone figure walked, head bent, and collar turned up against the icy wind. It was one o'clock on a bleak December morning and Jimmy was on his way home from work. Numbed with the cold he watched a flashing neon light and remembered how wonderful it had all seemed in September. Even during those first weeks of disappointment and humiliation, the warm sun and shining streets were like a fairy tale. He had been optimistic, sure he'd get a job before his money ran out. When it became obvious that a teaching job was out of the question, he had tried the Civil Service. They wouldn't even let him take the examination–he was too well qualified, they said, for a clerical job.

Gradually he lowered his demands. As his money ran out his visits to the 'Manpower' office became desperate. Daily he searched the newspapers, made phone calls, waited for hours in waiting rooms, filled out endless application forms and senseless I.Q. tests. Always with the same results: 'Sorry, you do not have Canadian experience.'

Nobody could tell him how he was to acquire this experience if he couldn't get a job. Then came the final degradation–applying for a job as a hotel porter. He was lucky he got it, and with tips he was financially better off than he had been at home.

Yet now he lived constantly with nostalgia, and all the ole-talk with the boys centred around the next trip home. The very things which had annoyed him now became infinitely precious. The disregard for time, the laughing informality, were symbols of friendliness in an unfriendly city. The other things like poor sanitation and bad roads became in retrospect symbolic of his own non-involvement. There were things wrong at home, certainly, but was he helping to correct them by living in North America? Next year perhaps he would get a teaching job, but at best he would always be an alien; he and the boys clinging together in a strange city trying to maintain their identity as Trinidadians! The thing was, it took a lot of courage to go home and admit you'd been wrong, and most of them balked at that.

Jimmy raised his head to face the icy wind and remembered week-ends at Maracas with the hot sun and the sparkling sea. Tonight when he got to the apartment he was going to write a letter. Maybe he could get his old job back. He was a Trinidadian, born to live in a warm climate with warm, vital people. There was no shame in that. This time he wouldn't just grouse about things. He would do what he could to help. Maybe he wouldn't be able to change things for a long, long time, but at least he'd be trying, and most of all he'd be helping to make his own country a better place to live in.

Jimmy smiled now at the thought of going back home. He pictured Piarco as it had been on the day he left for Toronto – jammed full of people! He hoped that they would all be there to meet him on his return!

IDA RAMESAR

Time for Talking and Writing

1. What was Jimmy's job in Trinidad? Point out *one* thing which showed that he lived comfortably.
2. What were some of the bad conditions in the island that bothered Jimmy as he became restless?
3. What are *two* important routine things which Jimmy had to do before he got a visa to go to Canada?
4. Why did Jimmy choose to go to Canada in particular and where exactly was he going to in Canada?
5. What was his 'send off' at Piarco like? Compare the airport at Piarco with that in Toronto.
6. Vishnu and the boys in Toronto can be recognised easily as Trinidadians. How did you recognise them as such?
7. What were some of the luxuries which Jimmy saw on his first night in Toronto?
8. What job did Jimmy settle for? Most of the places to which he applied for a job in Canada required a particular thing. What was that?
9. Pick out *four* things which Jimmy did regularly in his search for a Canadian job.

10. Jimmy's extra earnings on his job in Canada gave him more money than he earned in Trinidad. What did he miss about Trinidad? What did he hate about city life in Canada?

11. Do you think Jimmy was a coward for the decision he came to finally? Give reasons for your opinions.

12. Pick out the *true* and *false* statements and say why they are true or false.
    (i) Jimmy wasn't really qualified so he found difficulty in getting a Canadian job.
    (ii) Vishnu lived in a large house which he bought in Toronto.
    (iii) Jimmy was planning to return to Trinidad.

13. We hear a lot about the 'brain drain' in Trinidad. Find out what that means. Who or what was responsible for Jimmy's decision to go to Canada?

14. Would you advise a friend of yours to stay at home and live and work? Or do you think people should seek jobs in foreign countries? Give good reasons for your opinions.

15. Which of the following ideas is the writer of this story trying to leave with us?
    (i) Canada is an evil place.
    (ii) Trinidad is the best place in the world.
    (iii) One has to know the problems of living abroad before one decides to settle there.
    (iv) One needs courage to live away from one's home.

16. See if you can suggest another title for this story.

Chung Lee

Chung Lee, propped on his thin elbows, leaned over the counter, his chin resting dejectedly between his cupped hands. A cigarette hung limply from his lips. Old Su-Tang sat near him, silently puffing at his cigarette.

Trade was bad, very bad for Chung Lee these days; had been, in fact, for some months now. Why, he remembered the time when everybody in the village had bought their goods from him. Chung Lee always had everything. What busy days those had been for him! But that was before the big rich man had opened the store higher up the street. 'The Modern Grocery' they called it, and it was well stocked with everything. Chung Lee still had everything too, but scarcely anyone bought from him now. They all flocked to the Modern Grocery.

Every day he saw them pass. At first, feeling half-ashamed, they would slip by quickly, hoping Chung Lee had not seen. Then gradually they ceased to care. Who was Chung Lee anyway? Just an old Chinaman who couldn't speak English very well. They passed now boldly before his open doors, seldom even worrying to glance his way. Occasionally, when they wanted something in a hurry, and could not spare the time to go higher up the street for it, they would come in and buy, perhaps a pound of sugar, or an ounce of butter; never anything much. And always, without complaining, he gave them what they asked for.

Sometimes old Su-Tang would come in and keep his company. Together they would sit and smoke and talk. Time was when he never had chance for that. Too busy serving his customers! Now he was glad when Su-Tang came.

It was Su-Tang who had told him how many attendants they had up there at that other store; attendants all dressed in spick-and-span uniforms. Chung Lee looked down at his own torn vest. He needed a new one. But no customers;

Together they would sit and smoke and talk.

15

no money to buy one just now. Up there the floor was paved with pretty tiles. His floor was old now. The boards creaked as you walked upon them. Up there they had a whirring machine which cut thin slices of bacon. He had no such thing.

Yes, Su-Tang had told him all. He himself had never been there, would never go there. He would stay in his own shop, keeping the doors open as long as he could.

Mary Atkins came briskly up the street. It was Monday morning, and she had left the clothes soaking in the tub at home. She wanted half a bar of soap. She had forgotten to buy it from 'the Grocery' last Saturday. She would just step in at Chung Lee and get it quickly. She had a lot of work to do today.

Chung Lee saw her coming. It was Mary Atkins who, in those first days when the new store opened, had flounced by on her way there.

'Chinaman want new shop now too,' she had laughed as she passed. He had heard her himself.

Chung Lee puffed at his cigarette, and turned to Su-Tang.

'Y'know,' he said. 'I gi' you tip. Milk velly scarce soon. One time one body get six tin, eight tin, much as dem want. Soon one body get one tin. No mo'. No ship come in long time.'

Su-Tang shook his head sadly.

'Dis war! Nobody get much nothing.'

'Chung Lee, morning,' Mary Atkins said.

'Mawning,' Chung Lee returned, and went on talking to Su-Tang.

'Me have couple case lef'. Who buy someting else get milk. No buy someting else, no milk. Got to do so. Milk velly scarce soon.'

He turned to Mary Atkins.

'Wha' you want?'

'Half bar soap.'

Chung Lee laid it on the counter. 'Wha' next?'

'A pound sugar.'

'Nex' ting?' he asked, weighing and folding the sugar.

'Two tins o' milk.'

Chung Lee took one tin from the shelf, and placed it resolutely beside the other two parcels.

'Body buy plenty tings, mo' milk. Few tings, lil milk. Milk velly scarce soon.'

'But Chung Lee, — '

'Tirty-nine cent,' cut in Chung Lee.

The woman gathered up her parcels, paid and left.

On her way back home she stopped for a moment to tell Liza Deane that milk was getting scarce. She had heard Chung Lee telling Su-Tang.

'Chung Lee only give me one tin, but he got more. You better buy some things and try and get some before all gone. I going back again too.'

Liza called her daughter.

'Finish see after this breakfast,' she said. 'I going up at Chung Lee for milk.'

By the time she reached Chung Lee's shop there were two other friends with her.

'A pound o' bacon, Chung Lee, two pounds o' flour, half pound o' pork, a tin grapefruit, and four tins o' milk.'

She got them.

'Y'know, Su-Tang—' Chung Lee attempted to resume the conversation which had been broken off by the women's entry.

'Come Chung Lee, I got to get home. I want two pounds o' corn meal, a pound o' salt meat, four pounds flour, a bottle cooking oil, and six tins o' milk.'

Chung Lee placed four tins beside the other goods, and turned to the next customer.

'You now.'

Next day when Su-Tang came, Chung Lee was too busy to talk to him. Su-Tang sat in the usual place, smoked two or three cigarettes, and then went home.

And it continued like that for the rest of the week. Chung Lee had never been so busy. Not even in the days before the new grocery was opened.

Late Saturday night he closed his shop doors. He was hot and tired; very, very tired. He had served so many customers that day. He fingered his torn old vest. It was wet with perspiration.

Chung Lee puffed at the cigarette between his lips, but it had gone out some time before. He threw it on the floor, undressed and went to bed.

'Must order mo' goods nex' week,' he thought. Mentally he checked off the things he would need. Rice, flour, sugar, corn meal, bacon, sausages, . . .milk?

Before him rose the vision of the many cases which for a long time had lain in the back of his shop with no one to buy them.

'Milk velly scarce soon!' He laughed softly, turned over and went to sleep.

UNDINE GIUSEPPI

Time for Talking and Writing

1. As the story opens, what mood or frame of mind is Chung Lee in? Pick out one word from paragraph one which conveys that mood effectively.
2. What did Chung Lee do to earn a living? Why were things going slow for him?
3. What details of Chung Lee's rival in trade did Su-Tang give?
4. Why did Mary Atkins decide on that occasion to buy a bar of soap from Chung Lee?
5. As soon as Chung Lee saw Mary Atkins coming into his place he put a plan into action. What was that plan, and how was he helped with it?
6. What effect did Chung Lee's conversation have on Mary Atkins?
7. How did Chung Lee impress upon Mary the importance of his 'surprise news'?
8. What did Mary do as soon as she left the shop?
9. What effect did Mary's report have on her friends? And how did they show their belief in Mary's news?
10. The mood of Chung Lee at the end of the story is different from that at the start of the story. In what way is his mood a changed one?

11. With whom is the writer of the story laughing and at whom does she smile?
12. Do you think Chung Lee is a dishonest man, a cunning salesman, a dangerous liar or just a businessman? Give reasons for your opinion.
13. We learn a few things about the attitude and behaviour of customers. Give one example of one such attitude and one example of a type of behaviour of the buying public.
14. Discuss among yourselves various gimmicks business-men use in your country for the purpose of encouraging the public to buy more.
15. Write two paragraphs on the good and bad effects of advertising in your country.

Give and Take

You know Babu, Mass' Bob? Used was to do a little day work for your grandfather, when the yard need clearing and so . . . Him have a little boy, one sweet little boy you see, skin smooth, smooth black, like velvet, and nice wavy hair. Miss Katie tell me them just find him in the shallow water topside the market. . . . Dead. Well sar! The father suffer with fits you know, and like father, like son. Seem like him go for a swim, and the fits take him. But is God in His mercy save him from further sins, for him was goin' dead in jail. Look ya, Mass' Bob, the little boy bad, him bad, him bad so tell! Every day at school him and the boys ketch fight.

Wonder where them tek him? Must be the hospital, for him and the father has was to sleep under the shelf dem in the market. Imagine, a able-body man like Babu, living all these years, and never lif' a finger to build a house. The foxes have holes, and the birds their nests.

Him feel it though. Miss Katie say, when them find the body, you could hear Babu bawl and holler from up the fort; and after him understand proper say the boy dead fe true, him wouldn't go near the body, only bawl and holler and cuss God.

You know is one thing I never do, Mass' Bob? Just the other day up at Jericho, lightning strike a woman what was feeding her baby, kill the woman, and kill the dog under the house, and the blessed infant unscratch!

Babu is a hard man though; him used to charge you grandfather all ten shillings just to chop this little acre. Nobody never see him laugh or anything; only today, Babu bawling and cussin' God. The sins of the father . . .

But is God in His mercy save the boy, for him was goin' dead in jail . . . The Lord giveth and the Lord taketh away . . .

Him have a little boy. . .

Breakfast soon ready you hear sar? You can wash you han' and all that. Breakfast soon ready.

ROBERT HENRY

Time for Talking and Writing

1. Who is the person talking to Mass' Bob? How do you know that?
2. List on separate lines four things we gather about Babu.
3. The person talking to Mass' Bob seems to have a fair knowledge of sayings from the Bible. Pick out *three* of those Biblical sayings.
4. This story has the dialect or local language of a particular West Indian island. Can you suggest to which West Indian island it belongs? Pick out any of those expressions which helped you to decide on the island.
5. Try to write *in your own words* the story told to Mass' Bob. Be sure you give a clear picture of what exactly happened.
6. Why do you think the local dialect is very suitable for this story?
7. Pick out the statements that are *true* and those that are *false*. On separate lines give reasons why they are true or false.
   (i) The speaker had just seen the little boy in the shallow water.
   (ii) Babu's little boy was well liked and that was why the speaker was telling Mass' Bob about the incident.
   (iii) Babu's son died of drowning.
   (iv) Babu cheated people.
8. If you were Mass' Bob would you feel sorry or happy about Babu's trouble? Why?

9. Why doesn't Mass' Bob stop the speaker from telling the story before he took his breakfast? What light does this throw on Mass' Bob's relationship and attitude to the speaker?
10. From the stories he relates what can you say about the character of the speaker? Is he funny, wise, stupid, a nuisance and bore or a good gossip? How do you know if the writer of the story would agree with you or not?

The Kite

It was a beautiful thing made of four squares of light tissue paper, red, yellow, green and white, stuck together into one large square that would fly in the air like a bird. Philip knew that his father had bought it from the Indian kite-seller round the corner for five cents. He had always wanted one of those kites that Ramdeen had in a little cage on the door of his thatched mud hut but his father would say to him:

'You're too small to fly a kite.'

But at seven Philip felt that he was big enough to have a kite; yes, and many other things besides. He dreamed of kites at night, flew them in his imagination, would stand for a long time looking almost tirelessly at the kites of the bigger boys floating in the air like ducks sitting in the water or darting through it almost as swift as stones from a slingshot and there were some kites that danced in the air like girls stepping delicately from stone to stone on the muddy road before the house when it rained.

He thought of kites so much that he decided, even at the risk of a licking, that he was going to have one.

Philip was under the house busy with paper, scissors, thread and flourpaste when his mother called:

'Philip! Philip!'

He did not answer but stopped with the scissors in his hand, the paper on the ground before him, waiting for he knew not what.

'Philip! Where are you?'

Philip felt a shudder. The tone of his mother's voice was angry. He heard her slippers flopping down the back steps and then saw her thin, brown legs coming around the house. He thought of hiding behind one of the pillars but just then she stooped and caught him red-handed.

'Come out from under there!' she ordered.

Philip crawled out with the scissors still clenched in his fingers, flour-paste smeared on his arms and trousers and a long strip of cloth sticking to his heel.

'What in heaven's name! Who gave you permission to go in my work-basket and take my thread and tracing paper? What is that you got sticking to your foot? My good linen sheet!'

Philip sensed immediately that her rage had gone to fever pitch.

'Your father will hear about this!'

She boxed his head, held him by the ear and dragged him from under the house and into the house through the kitchen.

Philip knew well how strict his father was. Once or twice already he had been at the receiving end of that thick, brown belt that looked so cold and vicious that it made him tremble just to look at it. He wondered without much choice in the decision how his father would treat him when he heard about how he was under the house making a kite and stripping a piece off a linen sheet for a tail.

But Philip liked his father in spite of this and though his punishment in the past had hurt he felt he never got more than he deserved. He had been naughty at times and forgetful. He hoped this time it wouldn't be too severe; prayed that by the time his father came his mother would have cooled down enough to mix a plea of leniency with her complaint against him.

'Philip!' his father called after supper. This was it. He went and stood before his father, his hands behind his back. His mother was standing beside his father looking, he thought, slightly less angry than when she had dragged him from under the house by his burning ear.

'Philip, your mother has told me some bad things about you.'

He watched his father's brown, hairy hand on the arm of the chair, the big, brown veins standing up and running along his arm until they disappeared under his rolled-up sleeve.

'You went into her work-basket and took her tracing paper and you even cut a strip off her good linen sheet. A linen sheet is an expensive item, boy, but the more serious thing is that you did not have any permission. I should flog you for this but I will not. Perhaps part of the blame is mine. You've been asking me for a kite for a long time and I've been telling you you're too little. But you've proved by this that you're big enough, or at least brave enough to have one. But don't let me hear anything like this again.'

On the following afternoon Philip went with his father to Ramdeen's hut to buy a kite. They returned home and under his father's supervision he put on the tail, a long piece of red-and-black typewriter ribbon, and adjusted the compass. Now, holding it firmly but carefully against his body, he set out for the savannah to fly it, the wind, as well as his own excitement, singing in his ears. In the pocket of his trousers he felt, as he ran, the reel of thread pressing against his thin thigh.

There were already a few kites in the air when he arrived at the savannah. A pure yellow one seemed to dominate the sky. It soared and mounted, darted and dived as if it possessed some wild spirit of life while its tail writhed and lashed under it.

Philip envied the boy who could manage a kite so beautifully. Then he saw the kite take height and swoop down swiftly, its tail rigid, close to a black-and-white one. The black-and-white seemed suddenly to lose its power in the air; the boy flying the yellow shouted 'Ai-O! Ai-O!' and the black-and-white drifted and sagged, drifted and sagged, helpless in the wind, losing height all the time, until finally it disappeared wih a dispiriting nod of the head behind some houses far out of the savannah.

'Ai-O! Ai-O!'

Philip's admiration of the boy with the yellow kite turned into fear and he moved to another part of the savannah to put up his kite. It took the wind easily and the long red-and-black typewriter ribbon tail streamed out beautifully under it.

It was then that Philip proved Ramdeen's reputation. His kite mounted, dived and rode on the wind in response to the slightest flick of his finger. Whatever he did, it responded unexpectedly and beautifully. He thought of the boy with the yellow kite with thin slivers of chipped glass in the tail which he used to cut the threads of the other kites, and he remembered the fate of the black-and-white one.

'Perhaps I can fly a kite as good, or perhaps even better than him,' he thought, as his kite frisked and danced in the sky.

He paid out more thread so that his four-square-coloured kite looked more like a thing of heaven than a thing of earth.

Suddenly, he gasped with fear. The yellow kite was coming like a square-headed snake with a lashing, venomous tail, veering towards him. Frantically he began to pull in his thread but the yellow kite was too quick for him and it was clear that he must stay in the air and out-manoeuvre him, pulling in his thread at the same time until he was safe again on the ground. Philip trembled to think that his kite was entirely unarmed for battle with neither 'zwill' in the tail or 'mange' on the thread.

The yellow dived, its tail rigid, the sun hitting upon the 'zwill' in the tail. Philip watched it coming and jerked his hand and his kite went skating away sideways just as the yellow, rising suddenly upward, made a loop with its tail that lashed out and straightened as the kite mounted.

His heart was pounding with fear and perspiration was streaming down his face as he pulled in more thread but the yellow was moving across swiftly again and banking for another attack.

Philip felt utterly hopeless. He saw the yellow kite make a sudden dart to the right and whip back viciously. Philip was sure that he was gone this time but his courage came back as he felt tension still on his thread and knew that the yellow had missed him.

He pulled in more thread. If his luck held he would be safe.

'O God,' he prayed, 'let him miss me again.'

The yellow did not rise to dive again but cut Philip's thread in a sudden, upward, sweeping flight.

Philip felt the thread go suddenly slack in his hand and saw his kite sag in the air like people do when someone hits them in the stomach.

'Ai-O! Ai-O!'

Philip watched, shocked and murder-angry, as his kite went spinning and drifting and falling, spinning and drifting and falling, until it landed and became entangled in a

The yellow cut Philip's thread.

tree far out, almost at the other end of the savannah. He stared at the tangle of thread at his feet.

A group of boys had gathered and were laughing at him. He turned, saw the boy with the yellow kite and rushed up to him.

'You! You!' He was so choked with rage the words of the curse which he felt in his breast could not come out.

The boy, his freckled face shining in the sun, looked down at him and grinned, showing a space where two front teeth were missing.

'You cut my kite!' Philip screamed at last. 'I'll . . . I'll kill you!'

'Go and learn to fly a kite,' the freckle-faced boy jeered. 'Never hear 'bout the Dragon? When the Dragon in the sky no other kite could fly,' he boasted.

If he were not so big, Philip thought, he would kill him, if only for the boast in his voice. But he turned and walked out of the savannah, leaving his reel of thread on the grass, only his rage keeping his tears from flowing there and then. He finished the way home running and saw his father standing at the gate smoking a cigarette.

'What's wrong, Philip? Where's your kite?' his father asked.

Then, suddenly, Philip's grief and anger burst and the tears came rushing down.

'Come inside,' his father said, resting his hand on Philip's head, 'and tell me all about it.'

On the following afternoon Philip was again in the savannah flying a kite. But this time his father had put 'zwill' in the tail as well as 'mange' on the thread.

'Now, son, don't be a coward,' his father coached him. 'Stay there and fight. This is a man's world. No dragon ever lasted forever. You are going to make your own kites now and I'll help you. Not until you have downed the Dragon will you get another of Ramdeen's kites.'

It was towards the end of the season during which Philip had lost no less than half a dozen kites to the Dragon. But he was now one of the regular brigade who had learned to take his beating. When he got down to the savannah the Dragon was already reigning in the air. It had the sky to itself and seemed to glory in its lone exaltation.

Sombre-faced, Philip put up his kite. This one was a deep red and it shook in the brisk, warm air as he held it before releasing it, its tail entangled in a tuft of grass. Suddenly, he let it go as if he had released a bird to the sky. The strong wind caught it and swept it quickly upward. It stood there, poised, not very high from the ground, trembling, anxious to spring into obedience.

Philip let out the thread and it mounted higher and higher. He tried it this way and that to see how it responded. A sudden jerk to the left and it ducked. Lifting his hand, he played the thread over his left shoulder and it mounted jerkily from side to side as if walking in the sky. One tug up and one down quick and it darted away sideways.

Slowly he saw the Dragon coming towards him. He was not afraid. He rehearsed the words his father had told him: 'No dragon can last forever'.

The Dragon dived suddenly at him and he darted away and stood swinging to and fro in the sky as if laughing and slightly exhilarated by the attack. Gradually, he brought his red kite round again. He would bait the Dragon. The two kites stood close to each other about the same level in the sky.

The Dragon made a little rush but went back to its former position, like a boxer feinting at his opponent. But the red kite had already ducked, taking no chances. Now, the Dragon was climbing quickly back up to the level again. It paused for a moment and a sudden jerk of Philip's hand sent the red stabbing at the Dragon. But the Dragon swerved making an enormous loop low in the sky. Then it rose, its yellow, snake-like head nodding jerkily from side to side, climbing up the sky. The kites stood for a long time close to each other.

Then, almost imperceptibly, the Dragon began moving again towards the red until it was almost upon it. Then, rising swiftly, its tail struck at it with a vicious leap. Philip did not expect this sudden manoeuvre. It was luck alone that saved him.

Immediately, he became angry with himself over his carelessness. He pulled on his thread hard to the left and he mounted, passing the Dragon swiftly. Then he tugged to the right. The red dived madly downwards. It was a wild, uncontrolled, vindictive thing. It was Philip up there, hating the boy with the freckle-face. It came swooping down by the Dragon, darted across, hesitated a little as its tail caught the Dragon's thread, then continued plunging down to earth.

The Dragon buckled in the sky then went spinning giddily, its tail looping over its thread, close to the kite, as if hiding its face. Philip's kite hit the ground with a thud but the Dragon was already a speck in the sky, drifting disconsolately towards the roofs of some houses far out beyond the savannah.

Philip ran to his kite. It was battered and torn but as he raised it, it seemed eager to take to the air again. He held the thread and it lifted itself into the sky, the tear at the side of it purring like an anxious wing in the wind. As it soared back into the sky Philip remembered what his father had promised:

'After you have downed the Dragon you will get another of Ramdeen's kites.'

Philip twisted his mouth scornfully. He looked at his kite, gay in the wind, red as a wounded warrior, a wild, full-blooded thing. As it sang to the brave altitudes he could feel the vibration in the thread. He would match it against the best in the cage on Ramdeen's door. Yes; he would match it with the best of them, both for beauty and cunning.

BARNABAS J. RAMON-FORTUNÉ

Time for Talking and Writing

1. 'You're too small to fly a kite.' How old was Philip when he had his first try at kite-making? Where was his hideout while he made his own kite?
2. What *three* things did he steal from his mother to make

his kite? How did she punish him when she found out what he had done?

3. Philip's father did not punish him for taking the things without asking. Instead the father decided to buy Philip a kite.
    (i) What is the father's reason for so doing?
    (ii) Where else in the story does the father show a helpful attitude?
    (iii) What do you think about Philip's father?

4. Where did Philip carry the kite bought from Ramdeen to fly? Why was there a good place to fly kites? Why are busy streets unfit places for flying kites?

5. What kind of luck did Philip have on his first kite flying experience? How do you feel for Philip? Why did he really react to his luck the way he did?

6. To whom did 'The Dragon' belong? Was that name a suitable one for that particular kite? Why do you say so?

7. (i) What urged Philip to fight back and prove his power over the Dragon?
    (ii) How many times during the season did Philip try to defeat the Dragon?
    (iii) What qualities in Philip were developed during those repeated failures to down the Dragon?

8. On the day Philip put up the deep red kite, he experienced anxious, bitter and very happy moments. What created these varying moods on that day?

9. What was the writer trying to achieve by such a detailed description of that experience with the red kite? Suppose the writer had just summed up the outcome of that day in a sentence, what would be lost?

10. (i) In several parts of this story the kites take on human qualities. Pick out at least *three* human qualities the kites seemed to have.
    (ii) The kites also seemed like animals. Name *two* animals they seemed like.

11. There are many pretty similes which describe the kites at various points in the story. Select *three* of these similes and say what those similes are really describing about the kites.

12. There is a single word in the final paragraph of this

story which tells very accurately how great the struggle of the red kite was. Pick out that word.

13. *Two* words in this story are put into single inverted commas although they are not part of direct speech. Say why this is done.

14. Look up the meanings of these words found in the story: leniency; dominate; out-manoeuvre; imperceptibly; vindictive; dispiriting; disconsolately.

15. In this story you can see the usual qualities of young boys. What are these qualities?

16. Are you happy for Philip at the end of the story? What particularly did you admire about him?

Horace's Luck

The sweepstake vendor accosted Horace as the latter was jostling his way through Frederick Street, and sang out, as sweepstake vendors did in those days before the National Lottery, that he was offering for sale the 'one and only' winning ticket.

Horace, scrutinising more closely the ticket that had literally been thrust into his reluctant hand, felt a throb of excitement when he saw that its number was 1331 in the series 'H'. He immediately passed across fifty cents and tucked the ticket safely into his wallet.

For Horace, you see, was by nature a superstitious person and instantly recalled that 13 was his lucky number. Had he not been born on February 13th? And had he not taken up his very first full-time appointment on the 13th of . . . He could not at the moment remember the exact month. Perhaps it was June or July. The precise month was not of importance, however. What really mattered was the date.

There was in addition the fact that he was now in his thirty-first year. 13 and 31, joined together, made 1331. And—how exciting! —the figures when reversed were the same.

Also, the series 'H'. The initial letter of his own name 'Horace' was 'H'. Well, that clinched the matter absolutely. There was, he felt, no doubt about the ultimate result. The winning number was his. There it lay, safe in his wallet. It was only a question of time now. Involuntarily, he blessed the sweepstake vendor. It was a lucky day for both of them.

Horace was not only superstitious; he was addicted to day-dreaming as well. As he proceeded on his way he began to reflect upon the many things he would be able to do with the money. He hoped earnestly it would not be less than $40,000. Payment on the last winning ticket by the Trinidad Turf Club had indeed been in excess of that sum. He recalled,

He immediately passed across fifty cents.

though, that the 'Sweep' had on that occasion been won by a syndicate of ten persons, each of whom had received little more than four thousand dollars. A mere bagatelle! In his case, however, he would not share the prize. The entire forty thousand must be his and his alone.

He would, of course, buy a nice posh car – a new Chevrolet – one of those long, stream-lined affairs. Also, he would purchase a house in some good locality. In addition, there were quite a few people he was eager to dazzle. His new-won wealth would provide the means . . .

As was his wont, he lost himself in his dreams. It was the sudden loud screeching of brakes that warned him, but alas, too late! He was tossed and dragged for several yards along the roadway, to the accompaniment of horror-stricken cries from the crowds of fellow-pedestrians.

Horace regained consciousness a full forty-eight hours later to discover himself lying bruised, battered and shaken, on a bed in one of the wards of the General Hospital.

It was Police Constable Jones who had conducted the on-the-spot inquiries. Taking out his note-book and pencil, the first action he performed was to jot down the number of the vehicle that had been involved in the accident. It was a taxi. The number? . . .H. 1331.

NEVILLE GIUSEPPI

Time for Talking and Writing

1. Where was Horace when he was approached by the sweepstake vendor?
2. How did the sweepstake vendor encourage people to buy a ticket?
3. Why at first glance was Horace excited by the ticket offered him?

4. How much did he pay for the ticket and how much did he hope he would win?
5. What made Horace feel sure he was really going to win that sweepstake? Do you personally feel that superstition can help you win or lose things?
6. Horace day-dreamed of many things he would buy if he won the Sweep. What were they? Write in *one* paragraph what you would do if you won the first prize of the National Lottery.
7. Horace's day-dreaming got him into trouble. How did that come about? Does day-dreaming get students into trouble in a class?
8. What was the number of the taxi that landed Horace in the hospital?
9. We want to chuckle at Horace even though we feel sorry for him. Why do we want to laugh at the end of the story?
10. At the beginning of the story and throughout the greater part of it we are led to feel that Horace could really have good luck. But the end of the story takes us by surprise. What luck does Horace have? Is that an effective ending? Why?

Mama's Theme Song

'Oh, Georgie, how you so rude?' That was Mama's theme song. There wasn't a day that Mama wasn't singing that song. 'You rude, eh?' 'How you so?' 'Lord, this child going to kill me!' I mean, a man can get tired of all this preachifying. What's so specially rude about a little run down the gully with the boys? Everybody did it! And stoning the mango trees—he wasn't the first to start stoning, after all! If it wasn't for that stupid Mrs Beach—she had to recognise him and tell Mama so that she could be waiting with the strap when he reached home. Big, fat, ugly old woman! He hated Mrs Beach.

And Mama certainly knew how to make the strap walk across a fellow's back! Yes, sir! Rubbing the tender skin and trying not to cry too loudly, Georgie wandered to the back verandah and sat on the steps. The cool concrete soothed his hot flesh and little by little the tears subsided. Tired out with crying, he leaned his cheek against the wall and looked through misty eyelashes at the backyard scene— the thick breadfruit tree, always bearing, half-hiding the graceful clump of bananas that lay behind, while over to the right stood their sole mango tree (which, shame of shames, had not borne yet for the season) and in between them all the host of little pepper and tomato plants that Papa took such delight in. For Georgie, it was all haloed with rainbows, this tiny back garden squeezed into a few square feet of the city's space.

A low, impatient sound from a nearby bedroom reminded Georgie that Papa was home. Ever so often work would be slack at the factory and some workers would be laid off.

'Why you always have to be one of them?' Mama would ask angrily when Papa came home with the unwelcome news. 'They don't seem to want you at all, at all. You must be well slack on the job why they so quick to lay you off.'

Tired out with crying, he leaned his cheek against the wall

Sometimes Papa would give some plausible-sounding reason, but most of the time he would not bother. He was convinced that his wife did not believe him. But I do, Georgie would say to himself with fierce loyalty. I know that malicious foreman don't like Papa at all. Never mind, Papa–he would look across at his beaten, humiliated father and try to send the words soundlessly, just with his eyes– never mind. One day I'll be somebody big and you won't have to be working in that old factory.

While he waited at home to be recalled to work, Papa would spend much of the time lying in bed with a little transistor radio at his ear. After reading the newspapers and maybe an old magazine or two, he would fold his hands behind his head and stare at the ceiling. The insecurity of their position while Papa was unemployed preyed on Mama's nerves. It was then that she was at her most wasp- ish. Beatings were especially frequent at such times.

Oh God, when Papa going to work again? I only ten now– years before I could get a job.

'No job for you!' Mama had said firmly when he had sug- gested doing little odd-jobs. 'One person in this house going to finish right through to high school is you, mister!' His getting good marks in school only pushed the chance of his helping Papa further and further away, it seemed to Georgie. Yet those report cards were a source of such joy to both Papa and Mama that Georgie felt compelled to keep working hard at his lessons. There was nothing he enjoyed more than the sight of Mama with her 'put on' face–an incongruous mixture of self-conscious modesty and irrepressible pride–showing his report cards to the neighbouring women at the back fence. Then after that, how could he let them down? Yet, as long as he was plug- ging away at school, how could he help Papa?

Suddenly, Georgie became aware of two facts–the dusk had fallen and he was no longer crying. He got up, dusting off the seat of his pants, and wandered inside somewhat reluctantly. There was no knowing what sort of mood Mama might be in.

'Ah, Mama's boy, you coming to help me?' As the warm voice and the arms folded about him, Georgie wondered for the umpteenth time if he would ever understand his mother. Although this was the usual end of every tiff between them, it never failed to take him by surprise. In her anger, the bright eyes would glare so fiercely that one could never imagine that face ever smiling again. Yet now, as he looked up from her bosom, how beautiful that same face! How warm the eyes! So had she held Papa all these years; so she held Georgie now.

Moving with a much lighter step, he went to help her with the preparations for supper. Greta, his younger sister and the only other child in the house, skipped around them. Greta never did anything, hated the very idea of work, but somehow it never seemed to bother Mama. Or anyone else.

'Georgiee, let me help you; I want to help, Georgiee.'

'Go 'way,' he begged. 'You know you always break something.'

'Mama, see Georgie won't let me help him!'

'Georgie!'

'All right, Mama, all right. Look,' he turned a firm face to Greta. 'Start cutting this up. Use the enamel plate. Watch your fingers! If you cut yourself, is your look-out.'

And he pretended to turn his back, but was really keeping an eye on her in case anything untoward should happen. Of course, Greta soon put down what she was doing and wandered back out of the kitchen. Greta was the last child that his parents intended to have. He knew this because he often heard them discussing the matter. At times when Papa was out of work, Mama never failed to thank the Lord that they had only two children to feed. Papa was fond of children and would have liked to have more, though, strangely enough, he came from a very small family. Mama, who was one of eleven children, was adamantly in favour of small families.

'We know that we can provide for two,' Georgie would hear her say. 'Even if, God forbid, you was to die, I could get a job and mind them. Two children ain't hard. But if you was to leave me with six, how I would manage? Eh? Tell me that!'

Papa found the argument unanswerable–Mama's arguments invariably were–and the number remained at two. But all the neighbourhood children knew him as a soft

touch. He found it hard to refuse a child anything. No
wonder, then, that Georgie adored him and Greta was
spoilt and babied.

At the dining-table, Papa ate slowly and seemed lost in
thought. They had hardly reached mid-way when Adassa,
a neighbour, knocked and walked in.

'Call for you, Fred,' she told Papa, but he had already
jumped up and was moving towards the door.

'Thanks, girl,' he said as he went past her out into the
night. Adassa gave a little laugh.

'Like he was expecting it,' she said to Mama, who smiled
and nodded. Mama's manner did not encourage Adassa to
linger and she took the hint.

'I ain't stopping, eh. Just come to call him. Okay, then.'
She left.

Mama disliked Adassa's 'show-off' ways, as she called
them. The woman's husband was a dock-worker and he
earned plenty of money by working overtime. Besides, he
brought home a lot of new stuff from the wharf. 'Ole thief!'
Mama would say scornfully.

'Now, girl, don't say that in front the children,' Papa
would urge gently, though he couldn't help smiling at the
same time. Adassa's home was full of nice things, all
relatively new. And she had the only telephone on their
street. She liked it this way because she got to know everybody's business and secretly she hoped that no one else
would ever install a telephone, though publicly she sometimes complained that 'me house is a tru-fare'.

Having to use Adassa's telephone was a sore point with
Mama. She did not envy the other woman her television
set or her thick, expensive bedspreads, but she hated having
to ask Adassa a favour, which was what using her telephone
amounted to. 'Like a little lappy-dog,' she would say when
trying to explain her attitude to Papa. Georgie thought her
attitude was foolish; he enjoyed accompanying her on the
very rare occasions when she had to use Adassa's telephone.
While Mama spoke into the telephone, he would look all
around the living-room and, through the open doors, into
the two bedrooms and kitchen. The house was always
extremely clean as Adassa had no children and took a pride
in keeping her showplace spotless.

This is what I want for Mama and Papa, he would think to himself. In his mind's eye, he saw Mama sitting on the fluffy white stool (did Adassa ever use it?) in front of the bureau, combing her hair in a leisurely fashion and smiling at her image in the mirror. Mama was so much nicer and prettier than Adassa that Georgie sometimes felt that their roles should be reversed. Mama belonged in a place like this. But then, instead of Papa, he would have that awful Mr Binns for a father. Georgie loathed Mr Binns, with his small sneaky eyes and his way of giving a little laugh as he rubbed his hands. Poor Mr Binns actually imagined that he was being very winning. The neighbourhood children knew better, though. They thought him mean and stingy and called him names behind his back.

As Papa re-entered the house, they could see the change in him.

'They taking you back on again?' Mama called out to him from the table.

'Better, girl, better!' Papa was smiling all over himself. They could feel the excitement in him. 'Jonesy came through at last.'

'Jonesy?' Mama asked.

'Jones Watson—in the restaurant. You don't remember him? He work in the big Palace Restaurant downtown and you know how long he promise to speak to the boss for me? Ah, boy!' Papa swung round a chair close to Mama, sat down and gripped her by the shoulders. 'Girl, this is it at last! Jones get promoted and right away he think of me. He doing the hiring now and he taking me on for more than I was getting at the factory. And no more lay-off! Think of it, girl! Boy, I glad to see the last of that foreman's back!'

There was wild excitement for a while. Even Mama, old sceptic as she was, could not hide her joy. She cleared the table in a happy dream, smiling slightly to herself. From the kitchen, where she was washing the dishes, Georgie could hear a faint humming. He thought that this was a splendid opportunity to slip down the road to see his friend, Syd. He had to share the good news with a real friend. Papa had by now gone into his bedroom to see what he had to wear to the new job and Greta had tailed after her mother into the kitchen.

Georgie had just reached the gate when a voice froze him in his tracks.

'Georgie!' It was Mama, dish towel in hand. 'And where do you think you're going this hour of the night?'

Poor Georgie could not say a word.

'March yourself back inside here right now! You lucky I in a good mood tonight.'

And as Georgie sat down at the dining-table and tried to get himself into the proper frame of mind to tackle his homework, he heard from the kitchen, above the rattle of pots and pans being put away, 'Lord, this boy going to kill me. He too rude!'

JOY MOORE

Time for Talking and Writing

1. What two things did Mama try hard to stop Georgie from doing?
2. Do you think Georgie was rude? What did Mama really mean by calling Georgie 'rude'? How was he punished by Mama?
3. How did Georgie comfort himself after his punishment?
4. Why did Georgie feel so deeply for his father?
5. What job was Papa employed at? Why did he often find himself with holidays?
6. Look carefully into the story and find out how Papa spent his spare time. Could he have been a lazy worker at the factory?
7. Why do you think Mama was so quarrelsome when Papa was not working?
8. How do you know that Mama cared a lot about Georgie's future? How did she show her pride in Georgie's efforts at school?

9. Mama tried to make up to Georgie soon after punishing him. How did she do that?
10. Why was Greta allowed to be lazy and thus become spoilt?
11. Do you think Mama's reason for planning her family was good? Why do you say so?
12. How did Mama feel about neighbour Adassa? Why was it necessary to be friends with Adassa?
13. How was Adassa able to have such a well-kept house with so many luxuries?
14. What news did Papa get over Adassa's phone? Why did that bring so much happiness to Papa? (Give *two* specific reasons.)
15. How was Georgie going to show his happiness over Papa's news? How was he prevented from doing so?
16. In what ways were Mama and Papa good parents to their children?
17. Write a paragraph giving reasons why you admire Georgie.

The Teddy Bear

The schoolhouse stood on a grass plot away from the other buildings. It was small and simple in design. It was made to accommodate not more than fifty children between the ages of five and ten years. Part of the building was used as quarters for the teacher.

Miss Jessie had been teaching there for the last ten years. She had impressed her personality on the school. No one in the small community would think of having another to replace her. She had become part of the school, its soul. Without her it was a dead thing.

However, Miss Jessie was a lonely person when the pupils had left for home. To her the nights were long, too long for a woman who lived alone. She was restless, and would look forward to the new dawn with anxiety. Nights held her secrets which she shared with no one, not even Mrs Kidman, who was her close friend.

'I love that little girl of yours, Mrs Kidman,' said Miss Jessie as the two women sat at tea that afternoon.

'That's very nice of you,' replied Mrs Kidman.

'Mary is intelligent beyond her age, the kind of child I would like to have if I were married,' said Miss Jessie.

'It is not too late, Miss Jessie. Someone may turn up soon,' Mrs Kidman suggested with a twinkle in her eyes.

Miss Jessie smiled and shook her head to indicate the doubt that was in her mind.

'Never. I have decided to live among children as a substitute,' declared Miss Jessie with an air of finality.

'Never say "never", my dear,' advised Mrs Kidman.

'I am almost middle-aged now,' said Miss Jessie.

'Oh, no!' exclaimed Mrs Kidman.

When Mrs Kidman returned home she told her husband she had a suspicion that Miss Jessie held a secret desire to be married. After all, she was a woman and could find her fulfilment in loving and being loved, in having children of her own.

Mr Kidman agreed but found greater interest in the papers he took out from his briefcase.

The following day began with all the excitement of a normal school day. The children were at play in the sunlight under a cloudless sky. Everything was alive. Even Miss Jessie was extraordinarily lively. When she called on the children to assemble on the open space she took part in the drill exercises that preceded entry to the classroom.

No one but Miss Jessie had particularly noticed the stranger who was standing outside the enclosure on the far side of the school building. He was military in stature and dressed in a plain close-fitting suit that reminded one of a pilot's uniform. It was difficult to place him in an age group. His hair was grey, but not the grey of age. Physically he was firm and alert. His eyes were piercingly sharp, indicating that the mind behind them was trained in hard discipline.

He turned sharply to the left and walked away without showing interest in the persons he passed. To the men and women on the street he was one of those visitors who were soon forgotten. They left no particular impression.

But when the stranger returned the following day and the next and stood on the same spot overlooking the playground of Miss Jessie's school, men and women began whispering to one another. They became curious. They wanted to know who he was. They began asking questions.

The children gathered in small groups on the lawn and pointed to him. Miss Jessie became interested and came out on the playground to have another good look at him.

A cold sensation ran through her entire body as the stranger turned sharply to the left and marched away. She tried hard to think clearly. Her mind was in a confused state. She ran into her room and tried to settle her nerves. Whatever she did was to no avail. She kept asking herself Who was he? Where was he from? Why had he come?

That evening Mrs Kidman visited Miss Jessie. She found

The stranger . . . stood on the same spot overlooking the playground of Miss Jessie's school.

her in a very pensive mood. And it took a woman of experience such as Mrs Kidman to get the depressed Miss Jessie to speak about the stranger.

'I am confused. I do not understand my feelings at this moment,' said Miss Jessie.

'You should not take this seriously,' advised Mrs Kidman sympathetically.

'I am terribly upset by his presence,' emphasised Miss Jessie.

'You are not involved,' said Mrs Kidman.

'I am. I am,' repeated Miss Jessie.

'Relax, my dear. The gentleman will not come again,' Mrs Kidman declared with conviction.

Miss Jessie was left alone with her thoughts. It was a long night, and in spite of Mrs Kidman's advice, the restless woman could not relax. It was Mrs Kidman who had said someone might turn up. But Miss Jessie was not really prepared for any change. She could feel a powerful influence operating. What would tomorrow bring?

The children assembled and Miss Jessie gave the order to enter the classroom. She had slept little during the night and had not the physical energy to go through the simple drill exercise with the children. They had just settled down to class work when Miss Jessie saw the stranger standing at the open door. He had in his hand a parcel wrapped in coloured paper and tied with a length of yellow ribbon.

Miss Jessie, seemingly unaffected, politely approached the man. But the pit-a-pat of her heart was faster than it was wont to be.

'You are welcome,' said Miss Jessie.

The stranger handed her the parcel.

Miss Jessie's heart turned over and over within her breast.

'Please give this gift to the little girl dressed in blue,' said the stranger. Then he raised his right hand and turned about.

Miss Jessie stood at the door and saw him pass through the gate.

When Mrs Kidman came to take home her daughter, Miss Jessie handed her the gift.

'This is for Mary. It was left here by the stranger.'

There was a questioning look in Miss Jessie's eyes. Mrs Kidman opened the parcel and handed the child a Teddy Bear.

On her return home Mrs Kidman told her husband of the incident. He was amused.

'Oh,' he remarked, 'now I know who the stranger was. His name is Jack Foster. He was a famous pilot.'

Mr Kidman shook his head.

'But why . . . ?' began Mrs Kidman.

'Why the Teddy Bear for Mary?' her husband finished the question himself.

'On his flights Jack Foster always carried the Teddy Bear which his little daughter had given him for luck. When he came back from one of his flights she was no longer there. Now he gives away Teddy Bears. He is not all there.'

C. ARNOLD THOMASOS

Time for Talking and Writing

1. How did Miss Jessie earn a living? How long had she done this particular job? And how old do you think she was?
2. Why, in spite of the children she met daily, were her nights full of restlessness?
3. What did Miss Jessie wish for secretly?
4. Do you think Mrs Kidman was really interested in Miss Jessie's welfare? How do you know?
5. On the morning after the chat with Mrs Kidman, Miss Jessie had a surprise. What was that surprise?
6. What surprised her at first disturbed her later on. Explain why that was so.
7. Miss Jessie felt 'involved' with the stranger. Can you

tell what the writer of the story, at this point, is suggesting about Miss Jessie?

8. For what reason did Jack Foster approach Miss Jessie? Pick out *two* details which show how Miss Jessie felt as that man approached her.

9. In what tone of voice would you have Miss Jessie say 'You are welcome'?

10. What was in the parcel Jack Foster brought and for whom was it intended?

11. What was the reason for giving the child that gift? Who supplied you with that information?

12. What particular part of Miss Jessie's life is the writer trying to call our attention to? How does a Teddy Bear help us to understand it all?

13. Do you pity Miss Jessie or are you amused or annoyed at the behaviour of this woman? Give reasons for your opinions.

14. In the final paragraph of this story we are told that when Jack Foster came back from one of his flights his little daughter 'was no longer there'. Where do you think she was? What do you think the writer means when he says of Jack Foster 'He is not all there'?

De Trip

'Oh Chrise, look de time. If ah not careful, de plane will go leave me. And dese days you carn even rely on B.W.I.A. to be late. Long ago you could afford to get up dere at ten o'clock for de nine o'clock flight, but not now–now dey leaving before time.

Well, at long last we ready to leave de house. Now dis mean we go have to hurry like mad–and you know how it always is on de Churchill Roosevelt, wit a lot a trucks driving in de middle a de road an' going at twenty five miles an hour.

Well, lemme check an' see if ah have everyting . . . passport, ticket (ah *mus'* have dat), suitcase keys, tax clearance, hanky, cologne–what else? yes, de sea-sick tablets, jus' in case, doan min' is air ah travelling by.

Lord, we going so fast, ah mightn' reach at all. Slow dung little bit, nuh. Look out! How you could expeck to overtake when a car coming in de opposite direction? You want to kill me before ah reach?

We reach de airport at last. Buh looka de crowd a people! Lord, a whole village turn out to see she orf. She mus' be going up to New York. See she have on she heavy coat and she boots already, doan min' is eighty degrees down here. And is summer up dere, too. She mus' be doan know right now up dere hotter dan down here.

Yes, you go and park de car while I go and push tru de line to de counter. Oh Gord, looka de crowd by de 'But Will It Arrive' gate! I know someting had to happen! Dey trying too hard to leave on time! How dey expeck to stand de strain?

Hey, look me here! Put de suitcase and dem right here. Not so far back, you idiot! You want me stand up here all day? Ease dem up some more, doan min' if dat wrinkle-up old red hen stare at you. Is to stare she back and push up de suitcase to de counter. She too polite to tell you anyting.

Well, yes, weigh dem good! Look at de time! You tink is now dey announcing dey want we to board? Look at dat, twenty minutes to go an' look how many people still here. How dey expeck you to board if you ain' check in yet? An' dat girl say she here since eight o'clock.

Yes, push de baggage on de scale now. Here me ticket and me two dollars . . . What you mean ah overweight? You see dat now—ah have to dig into me holiday money to pay people fuh stupidness. Here—and doan forget de tag—las' time you make me baggage go clean to New York. Doan try it again!

Well, boy, ah carn even stay an' chat little bit. Ah have to board now. So 'bye, sweetheart, an' take care an' doan spree too much—an' write me now, you rascal! Ah gorn! An' doan forget de pumpkin an' you mus' sweep de house, an' remember to bring in de garbage pan before somebody tief it, an' doan leh dem neighbours trow dey rubbish over by we—an' make sure an' put some ointment on dat cut. Bye!

Yes Sir, see all me documents here. Gate one dey say? All right, lemme try an' get a good window seat—one near de exit an' de toilet.

Well, ah reach orn at last, and looka de nice seat up near de toilet. Good! An' it on de right side, too. De sun carn get at me.

Is who dis coming to sit by me? Two young girls wit dey rackets. Dey mus' be going up de islands to play tennis. Buh look how dis one come and nearly brain me toe wit de racket! An' de handle lolling on me knee. She carn put it over by she? What she tink I name? Racket holder? Lemme jus' trow it over on she foot. Good! She get de message—she moving it!

Eh, eh, de plane moving. Wait till ah get me chair and me table straight. Right, ah ready fuh anyting now . . . Oh Lord, if dat stupid girl dig me in me side one more time, ah go break she ribs fuh she . . .

Well, look we flying over de Nodern Range! Oh Gord,

suppose de plane crash! Hush yuh mout, chile, you always expecking de worse. You see, an' talking to me self again! If people hear me now, dey go say ah crazy! Buh who to know what going orn in me brain?–An' ten-to-one dey talking to deyself too, buh only a fool like me would admit it.

Eh heh, de drinks coming roun' now. Buh is only tomato juice ah seeing. Me ain' warn no tomato juice, man. When dey come to me, ah going ask for orange juice instead.

Buh wait, like dey not coming my way wit de juice. No tanks, none a dem dry-up tarts fuh me. Ah want some juice . . . Chrise, why she so sour, de ole red hog? Like ah not good enough fuh she to serve! What she tink she getting pay fuh? To put orn nice clothes and say 'Tanks fuh flying wit us'? So wait, ah going have to siddown all de way from here till when de plane lan' wittout a ting to drink?

Wait, wah dat she announcing? Oh Gor, de plane dropping! We go dead! Wah dat she saying, chile? . . . What! Is only lan' we lan'ing? Dat is all? Well, it give me a fright, ah could tell you. Sorry ah hole orn to you so tight! Doan min' de finger marks. Dey go soon fade. Sorry again! . . . Chrise, like she ain' inten' to stop rubbing de place–like she say ah meant to do it!

Well, it look like we go really reach safe, fuh true. Ah only hope a tyre doan blow out or someting. Doan min' people does say ah look fuh trouble, you have to learn to expeck de unexpected.

Ah too hope we get down soon. Ah want to go somewhere, but dey say you stay in you seat till we lan'. Me too 'fraid to get up, anyway . . . Oh Lord, if ah doan go to de toilet soon, ah go shame meself!

Ah could get orf now? Tank de Lord fuh dat! Now is only de Customs to worry 'bout . . . Wait, Immigration firs'. An' look dey tell me ah could only stay seventeen days! Buh what is dis at all? I thought you could stay as long as you want! How you mean, only seventeen days? An' I have so much relatives to look up! You mus' be outa you min'! . . . All right, Sir, is you lan', not mines, so give me back me documents and leh me go an' collect me luggage.

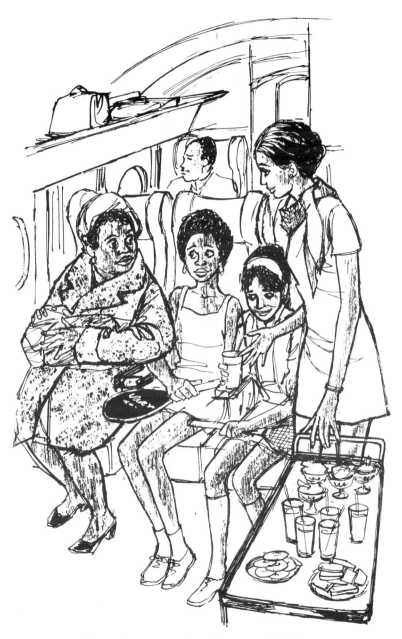

No tanks, none a dem dry-up tarts fuh me.

Oh Gord, looka suitcases! You tink ah could ever find mines in dis crush? Wait, look one a dem dere. An' dat Mister Man like he making orf wit de odder two! Hey . . . How you mean is yours? You trying to tell me I doan know me own luggage?

Tag? What tag? Whose name? You tryin' to fool me, nuh? I doan know nutting 'bout no tag wit name. You jus' now put dat orn. You mus' be tink ah is an ignorant traveller. . . Eh? Police? What police have to do wit dis? All right, if you say is yours, is yours–because ah tink ah jus' see mines over dere wit de piece a sticking plaster Tantie Jean use to patch de rip.

What ah have to declare? De farseness a de man! Is only me clothes in here! What you could want to open for? All right, ah have a couple roti too and some callaloo for me gran'mudder. Dat is all.

Mangoes? What mang. . .? Eh, eh, you know ah forget ah have dem? Nutting else, honest to Gord . . . excep' some bay rum and some guava jam.

Confiscake? Confiscake? Look, ah could pay you, you know. How you mean colleck on de way out? You! I know you! Colleck on de way out mean come an' get de empty bottle an' dem. Look, lemme siddown right here an' fill me belly. You could have de little what leave over.

Ahh-h. Urp! Now ah ready to fin' me people. . . . Cyntie, me chile, ah reach. Buh Chrise, you get fat! What you eating so? An' is so George look dry up.

An' who dis is? Is Urina so big? How old she is now? Ten already? Well, well, an' de larse time I see she she was only eight and look how much she grow in two years! Well, well, well!

Well, let's go orn home. Ah have plenty tings fuh allyou! You fin' ah looking well fat? Doan min' dat, chile. Dey search two a me grip, but ah have plenty tings hide in me udder one an' in me han' bag–an' if you see, presents under me dress! All up here so pack up wit tings! Come, leh we go home, leh me ornload!'

JOY CLARKE

Time for Talking and Writing

1. From the first two sections of this story can you say what the speaker is preparing to do? What details help you to know for sure?
2. There are two jokes in these two sections. See if you can pick them out.
3. Where is the speaker in section three? What is her main concern and difficulty there?
4. What is the speaker doing in section four?
5. Do you think this was the first plane trip to a foreign country the speaker was making? Why did you get that impression?
6. To what kind of country was the speaker travelling? How do you gather this information? For how long was she allowed to stay there?
7. Why did the speaker decide to eat the things she was carrying for her relatives?
8. What were the first things the speaker noted about her relatives living abroad?
9. This is a story which resembles a play with several scenes. In each scene of the story there are silent listeners. See if you can guess to whom the speaker is talking in each of these scenes.
10. We learn a lot about the type of person the speaker herself is from the things she says and does. Write down the qualities of her character you have discovered.
11. *Either*
   Think of the time between your leaving home for school one morning and the start of the first class of the day. Then invent for yourself three scenes in which you talk and make comments to silent listeners.
   Or
   Continue, if you can, this story by Mrs Clarke. Try to make comments the way you think the speaker would when she saw other people and places during her stay abroad.

The Hustlers

Scrape, scrape, scrape-scrape! The sharp sounds aroused Mr Grasper from his restless sleep.

Someone was scraping his jalousie windows with a stick. He recognised the sound only too well, for it was a sound he always welcomed in the dead of the night.

'Who there?' he shouted.

'Tis me, Sonnie Boy,' a voice shouted back.

'What you want?' inquired Mr Grasper.

The voice called back, 'You know it could be only one thing I would call you fo' at dis time o' night. I come to tell you dat ole man Gussie Smith deading.'

Mr Grasper was one of the two undertakers in the village, and there was, naturally, bitter enmity between himself and the other–Mr Grabbit. In fact, the spirit of competition was such that the village lads made pocket money by selling first-hand information to them when anyone in the village was expected to pass into the Great Beyond.

To make matters worse the inhabitants of the village held on to life with the greatest tenacity. So when the Angel of Death hovered over anyone, it was likely that both Mr Grasper and Mr Grabbit would be there.

Now, Mr Grasper lost no time in getting ready; indeed it seemed as if he had slept in his clothes so as to be prepared for any such emergency, for in a matter of minutes he stepped fully dressed into the night and joined Sonnie Boy.

'Well,' he said, 'Sonnie Boy, I am mightily glad you came for me instead of going for Grabbit–he too grasping!'

'Dat ain't nutting,' replied Sonnie Boy. 'Sylvester done gone fo' Mr Grabbit but doan let dat bodder you, I know a short cut dat would get you dere before dem; but it going cost yo' a little extra.'

'Well,' replied Mr Grasper in a business-like tone, 'two dollars is a deal?'

'Mr Grasper, dat doan suit me,' said Sonnie Boy very emphatically. 'Three dollars fuh coming to tell you, an' a dollar for de short cut. To besides, I had to leave me warm bed to come out in de cold night to tell you dat Mr Gussie did deading. No such; four dollars or nutting doing.'

Mr Grasper was desperate. He knew Sonnie Boy had not come out of a warm bed; in fact he doubted whether Sonnie Boy had a bed at all. But that did not alter the situation, and so Mr Grasper tried again. 'Let us make a deal: three-fifty. I am a poor man and I ain't had a "turn-out" for four months. You know, people in dis village doan die regular.'

Sonnie Boy smiled to himself. 'Look, Mr Grasper, you gwine let fifty cents mek you loss de "turn-out"? Mek up you mind and done. I can't stan' out in de dew arguing wid you de whole night.'

Mr Grasper knew only too well that if he did not pay the amount asked for he would not be able to rely on Sonnie Boy to bring him welcome news in the future, and in frustration he cried, 'O.K., O.K., let us go!'

'Hold me hand. I can pull you 'long faster dan you kin run,' suggested Sonnie Boy. Mr Grasper held on to Sonnie Boy's hand for dear life and together they raced through fields of banana trees until they reached the yard of a low-slung bungalow.

Mr Grasper was panting and gasping for breath, but there, in the semi-darkness, he discerned the portly figure of Mr Grabbit struggling towards the house, and with a sudden burst of energy he ran forward and reached the top step of the veranda just as Mr Grabbit reached the bottom step. It was indeed a race to the death!

In all fairness, it would have seemed that Mr Grasper had won, but Mr Grabbit refused to admit defeat.

'I ain't leaving until de family decide which of we going bury de dead,' he announced to Mr Grasper.

Mr Grasper ignored him. He straightened his tie, adjusted his beaver more firmly on his head, and knocked at the door.

The door was opened by Mr Gussie Smith's daughter. 'Come in, Mr Grasper and Mr Grabbit, come in, both of you. Pappy is dead already.'

Mr Grasper smiled the sickly smile he thought expressed

A race to the death!

his embarrassment at having to perform such sad duties. 'Miss Connie,' he purred, 'seeing I am reach first, it means "Prompt Service".'

Mr Grabbit promptly joined in, 'Miss, kindly let me express my deepest sympathy (a tear rolled slowly down his cheek). I delayed a bit, knowing that you would wish for a little time to pray at the side of your loving departed; he was a dear, dear friend of mine, and I always had the greatest respect for him, therefore I do not intrude, but you know "Courtesy and Efficiency" has always been my motto.'

Miss Connie smiled sadly, 'I doan know what to do; Pappy always said "Come first, served first". Oh dear, I just doan know what to do! The best thing is for both of you to look at the body and decide what you would charge to bury him, and then I will choose the best "turn-out" for the littlest amount of money.'

Mr Grasper interposed, 'Miss Connie, my "turn-out" is the best, most modern and up-to-date.' Mr Grabbit joined in by saying, 'Mr Gussie is an old man, and old-fashioned, and I know that if he could choose, he would choose a "horse-hearse" and I still got one.'

'Never mind what you think, you both do what I tell you,' Miss Connie said. 'He is in that room,' pointing to a door.

The two undertakers entered the bedroom, Mr Grasper's beaver sitting firmly on his head, while Mr Grabbit's Fedora tilted at a precarious angle.

In the room an oil-lamp burned low and cast eerie shadows on the body lying on the bed, reflecting from the eye sockets a golden glow.

Mr Grasper rubbed the palms of his hands together, while Mr Grabbit pulled thoughtfully at his chin. Suddenly both realised that Pappy Gussie's eyes were weighted by sovereigns!

As everyone knows, sovereigns are very, very rare and both of the undertakers' minds ran along identical tracks. Both made simultaneous darts for the coins. Mr Grasper grabbed for the one on the right eye, and Mr Grabbit grasped for the one on the left eye.

At this juncture a terrible voice came from the corpse. 'Left dem, you teefing carron-crow; robbing de dead, will yo'?'

Mr Grabbit sat heavily on the floor, his Fedora slipping and sitting on his ear. Mr Grasper remained, as if frozen, in a bending position, his hand poised in mid-air.

The corpse sat up and chuckled maliciously. 'I know I did going catch wunnah,' it croaked. 'Wunnah won't learn to let a poor body dead in peace before wunnah fight over he. I mek up me mind to teach wunnah a lesson. Give de dead a little time to get reconcile to de odder side first before wunnah rush in.'

Old man Gussie Smith raised his voice, 'Sonnie Boy and Sylvester, all two-o-you, come in.'

The two boys walked in, their faces convulsed with laughter. 'Here,' Gussie Smith said, handing them each two dollars, 'dis is what I promise you if you get dese two carron-crow here.'

Sonnie Boy turned to Mr Grasper. 'Whey de four dollar you arrange to pay me?'

Mr Grasper recovered himself. 'Not one blind cent, you outlorded tief,' he raged.

Mr Grabbit was having the same trouble with Sylvester. 'Dis is robbery,' he shouted, getting up from the floor and dusting the seat of his trousers.

Mr Gussie Smith chimed in, 'Well, boys, doan bodder wid dem. If dey pay you, keep all-you mouth shut 'bout tonight; if dey doan pay, spread it all 'bout de village.'

There was a rustle of notes and two heavy sighs as the undertakers paid up.

FLORA SPENCER

Time for Talking and Writing

1. There are really *two* pairs of hustlers in the story. Who are they? What do they hustle after?

2. Who is the better businessman, Mr Grasper or Sonnie Boy? Why do you think so? What deal do these two make? Why does Sonnie Boy succeed quickly?
3. How is Mr Grasper able to reach the bungalow first?
4. The writer says Mr Grasper and Mr Grabbit made 'a race to the death'. Can you explain this statement?
5. Mr Grasper and Mr Grabbit are good actors. They can 'bring off' well. How do they 'bring off' at Miss Connie's bungalow?
6. Miss Connie leads these two hustlers into a trap. How does she do that?
7. The eyes of the dead man shone brightly. How was that possible?
8. The greediness of the hustlers took over immediately after they saw the dead man. Is this true? Why?
9. Gussie Smith rose from the dead. What was the effect of this on Mr Grasper and Mr Grabbit? Why didn't they run away?
10. Sonnie Boy and Sylvester made a profit on the whole business. How much did each get eventually and from whom did they get this money?
11. How could Mr Grasper and Mr Grabbit become ruined men? What is the word we give to ruin caused in that way?
12. Suppose we called the story *Profit and Loss*? How would this title suit what happens in the story?
13. Although the story points out a serious situation, it makes us laugh a lot. Where do we laugh and why are those parts of the story funny?
14. The story starts with sounds someone is making with a stick. Why is that a good way to begin a story? The end of the story is suggested by other sounds. What are those sounds? Why is it good to suggest an outcome instead of telling it directly?
15. Village life is full of colour and comedy. What has the Government in your country done to bring out and preserve some of these qualities?

Journey by Night

He stood alone, leaning against a post, and shifting his weight from one foot to the other. It was late, and the taxi-stand was empty. The street was silent. He looked up and down, hoping that some vehicle would come in sight, for he wanted to get home. But none came.

The silence began to pall. He started to whistle, but there was no mirth in it, and he soon stopped. Midnight, ten miles away from home! What was he to do? To begin to walk that distance was out of the question.

A dark cloud passed across the sky, hiding the few pale stars that had been there. The noise of a falling dust-bin reached his ear. Some dog must have been scattering its contents.

Instinctively his hand felt for his wallet. Yes, it was still there. If only he had a stick! But he had nothing with which he might protect himself. He began to walk up and down, up and down.

What was that in the distance? At last two headlights were drawing near. He stepped into the middle of the street and held up his hand, and the car stopped.

'Taxi?' he asked. 'Valencia?'

'Get in,' said the driver, opening the door.

He sat beside the driver, glad to be on his way home at last. He had felt so lonely while he had been waiting. If only someone would say something! In the semi-darkness of the car he turned to look at the other passengers, but no one else was there.

The driver said nothing to him as the car sped along.

Suppose . . .

No, he mustn't allow himself to think of that. He glanced at the driver, and again his hand went to his wallet. He had heard of passengers being attacked at night and robbed. But surely . . . No, that couldn't happen to him.

He stepped into the middle of the street and held up his hand.

If only he could see the other man's face clearly! But he had no idea who the driver was. He kept his eye intently on him during the seemingly interminable journey.

Now they were approaching a spot where the road branched off in another direction. There were tall, dark bushes around. The car slowed down, and the driver was looking at him. Then the driver took something short and black from the side-pocket of the car. It looked like an iron tool. Would the driver attack him with that?

'Stop!' he heard himself screaming, and his heart beat so fast with fear that he could hardly breathe.

But the car did not stop. Faster and faster instead it went. Now they were nearing his destination. Did the driver intend to take him past and then . . .

'Put me down here,' he cried out.

Still with his eyes on the driver, he quickly stepped from the car as it came to a standstill. He fumbled in his wallet for his fare, but the taxi was no longer there.

'No night passengers for me again,' exclaimed the driver, as with a sigh of relief he hurriedly moved off. And his hand tenderly caressed the heavy spanner with which he had meant to defend himself had that queer passenger attacked him.

UNDINE GIUSEPPI

Time for Talking and Writing

1. At what time of the night was the passenger waiting for a taxi? Pick out *three* details which help to create the time of the night.
2. What *three* things can you note about the passenger? Use three separate lines for your answer.
3. How many other people were there in the car?

4. In what ways does the passenger show his fear while sitting in the car?

5. Just before the story ends, the writer builds up tension or anxiety. Pick out the various actions which help, step by step, to create that anxiety.

6. Very often a good short story has an unexpected ending. In this story what makes the end unexpected?

7. Driving in the dark can be as frightening as walking alone in the dark. In *one* paragraph describe a quick walk you made one night. See if you, too, can build up, step by step, anxiety and fear. Remember sounds, images and feelings can do a lot to create the fear.

8. If you were a driver would you stop for a passenger at midnight? Why?

9. In paragraph four find one word which can mean *acting without anyone advising*.
   In paragraph eleven find one word that means *in a secret way*.
   In paragraph twelve find one word that means *endlessly long*.

10. Why do you think there are dots after the paragraphs: 'Suppose . . . ' and 'Did the driver intend to take him past and then . . . '?

The New Teacher

We bade our English master, Mr Ramsawak, a solemn farewell. Tall, lean and greying, Mr Ramsawak had taught at the school for many long years, and he was a favourite with everybody. Now he was retiring. He had reached the age limit.

As usual on such occasions, the girls had shed their tears during the function which had consisted of the singing of a couple of Indian and English songs, a few speeches, and the presentation of a gift.

The General Certificate of Education examination was only a few months away, and everyone was worried about having to change a teacher, especially an English one. Mr Ramsawak had been somewhat old-fashioned in his methods of teaching, perhaps. He believed that his students should have a thorough knowledge of formal grammar, and throughout his career he had drilled them regularly in the many various rules.

He himself spoke elegant English, and he insisted that we should do the same. Somehow or other, year after year, the percentage of passes in his subject had generally been higher than in many of the other subjects taught in the school. Mr Ramsawak was considered a good teacher!

His successor arrived two days after Mr Ramsawak had left. His first class was the Fifth Form—my class, and so I had my first meeting with the new teacher.

As he entered the classroom, I observed that he was a young man. His well-coiffured hair hung down to his shoulders. His penetrating, brown eyes focused on us; his voice was slightly metallic. But what fascinated us most about him was his manner of speech. It was—to say the least—unexpected!

He paced from one end of the room to the other.

'Ah name Ramoudit Singh; ah was born on de 30th

My first meeting with the new teacher.

December, 1950; ah come out from San Fernando. As all yuh know, ah come to teach English language, buh as all yuh will find out, ah believes in talking de language of de people. Dat way all yuh understan' mih, an' ah understan' all yuh. Right?'

He paused, and looked at us intently.

'Ah know all yuh ain't too happy wid mih cutting in at dis present time, especially as dis is mih fust job, and wid English exam coming up just now, buh we go have to try to get along and see wha' we could do. Right?'

He resumed his pacing. He held the attention of the entire class. Eyes followed him from one place to another and back again as he retraced a steady path. Utter silence from us students prevailed for that entire period. What was happening was unbelievable, but it was true.

'Ah ain't no bright man,' the new teacher continued, 'an' ah doh like people who feel dey hah too much in dey head. An nex' ting, doh feel all yuh inferior to mih, even doh ah hah mih G.C.E. O-Level, and all yuh ain't. We equal. De only ting is dat all yuh sitting down dey, an' I stannin' up here. Ah ain't really hah no more dan yuh, an' yuh ain't hah no more dan me. If yuh shy, ah doh believe we go get along, fuh in English we hah to convey ideas to each odder. An' we mus' convey dem in we mudder-tongue. Leave de fancy style fuh writin'. In any case, yuh won't hah much uses fuh dat wen yuh leave school, cause is here in yuh own country we wants yuh to stay.'

Mr Ramoudit Singh was fluent on the subject of West Indians remaining at home. 'Wha' all yuh want wid white people country and white people language?'

For a fleeting moment I thought of Mr Ramsawak.

When the bell rang, and the new teacher left the class-room, the uproar was deafening. Mr Ramoudit Singh was the inevitable subject of conversation.

During his second lesson with my class, the new teacher hardly spoke. He listened instead. He implied that this was to enable him to assess the standard of *our* English. Towards the end of the lesson he made his comments.

'De vocabulary ain't too wide, grammar O.K., ideas good, buh need more developing.'

It was on his third day, however, that he surprised the

class. He handed out Xerox copies of a passage for comprehension. In order to save time, oral questions and answers were to follow. The passage was one of the most beautifully-written bits of prose I had read for a long time.

'Is I self write dat wen ah was at school,' Mr Ramoudit Singh claimed, 'an' now ah go ask all yuh questions to see if all yuh understan' it.'

I found it difficult to associate the passage with Mr Ramoudit Singh, and with the questions he began to ask in the 'mudder-tongue'.

Visions of Mr Ramsawak rose before me once again.

Concerned as we all were about the possible results of our coming examination, I was forced to wonder which posed the greater problem – translating 'English-as-written' into the 'mudder-tongue' for purposes of speech, or translating the 'mudder-tongue' into 'English-as-written' for exams and for communicating with the rest of the English-speaking world?

Only a longer exposure to Mr Ramoudit Singh's methods of teaching would provide the answer. And if he proved to be a less successful teacher than Mr Ramsawak had been, it probably wouldn't matter, anyway.

'Cause', as Mr Ramoudit Singh had pointed out, 'is here in yuh own country we wants yuh to stay.'

NINNIE SEEREERAM

Time for Talking and Writing

1. Why did Mr Ramsawak have to leave the school?
2. What subject did he teach?
3. Was the school in the story a Primary or Secondary school? How do you know?
4. How did Mr Ramsawak prepare his students for the exam?

71

5. Do you think Mr Ramsawak was a successful teacher?
6. How did the new teacher stand out as a distinct contrast to the old teacher?
7. During his first lesson, the new teacher, Mr Ramoudit Singh, made a few points about the subject he was going to teach. Put in your own words *three* of those points.
8. How did Mr Ramoudit Singh carry out his second lesson? What conclusion about the class did he arrive at? Why do you think that was a good way to start teaching a strange group of children?
9. Mr Ramoudit Singh had tried to make the teaching of English helpful and worthwhile. Give two ways in which he tried to do so.
10. Do you think more students would have passed the exam under the new method of Mr Ramoudit Singh? Give your reasons for your opinion.
11. What did Mr Ramsawak want from the students? What did Mr Ramoudit Singh want from them?
12. The writer of this story feels that if we learnt only our local dialect as 'English' we might face a problem. What problem is that?
13. How can the use of our local dialect in the classroom help students? Be specific.
14. In what way could Mr Ramoudit Singh fail and why? In what way could he succeed and why?
15. What qualities of Mr Ramoudit Singh do you personally admire and what do you dislike? Give reasons for your suggestions. Do you think the writer of this story would agree with what you think?

Up the Wind
Laka Notoo-Boy

There was no man in our little village who was more feared than Chester. Looking at him, a stranger could never understand why an entire village should live in fear and trembling at such a man. His outer skin clung to his bony framework with the jealousy of a postage stamp and the older villagers claimed that in all his years nothing ever came between these two. His clothing, as we called it for want of a better name, hung on him by accident and the entire village marvelled that the accident had not actually happened yet. Everyone knew it was bound to happen sooner or later. It was just a question of time. The story even went the rounds that Chester had stopped taking off these clothes for fear that he could never put them together again. The most recent development of this was that even when he slept he did not change his clothing and if he needed to turn in his sleep he would raise himself to a standing position, turn, and then go back to sleep.

Some people attributed the most notorious character to Chester. His slight limp was attributed to the fact that when he first came to the village, he had just been driven out of another village because he dabbled in witchcraft. The villagers there had beaten him so badly that he remained with a limp for the remainder of his life.

The older people said he moved quietly into the village so that before anybody knew it he was a villager living in self-imposed exile among the cenrida trees. He built his hut single-handedly and daubed it himself.

His achievement was all the more marvellous because he had only one hand that was capable of use. His left hand seemed to have been twisted in paralysis, but the villagers had a story for that too.

The story was that Chester was a man who had returned from the dead: in his previous village people had seen him die and rise again. His first miraculous power explained how he built his house single-handedly and all the other powers attributed to him. The true story was that Chester was diabetic, a secret which he guarded jealously and when he fell into a deep coma everybody thought him dead. After two days and nights of wake, rum, coffee, biscuits and hymns, the corpse was heard to groan. The brave remained to ensure that Chester really groaned. The remainder, atheist, agnostic and believer fled in panic, creating new passages through the walls as they went. When Chester was next seen, his left hand hung closely to his side and villagers shunned him. Some said he was being placed in the coffin when he groaned, others claimed he was already in the coffin and the lid was sealed when he rapped with his left hand and that caused his hand to be as it was.

Whatever the reason, our entire village lived in mortal fear of that left arm. We had heard stories of the devastating effect it had on those who dared to enrage Chester, a task which anyone could do with no real effort.

For us children, Chester was everything. He was our village champion in our rivalry with our counterparts in the neighbouring village. Once his name was mentioned they conceded they had no such thing in their village. Our parents constantly left home when we did anything wrong and went to report to Chester. For days after, we remained indoors seeking a hiding place at the mere mention of the name 'Chester'.

Everybody soon learnt about Chester's temper but in spite of our fear we could not resist the opportunity to tease Chester on our way to or from school. The size of our groups added strength to our hearts. Everyone attempted to outdo the other in shouting 'Up di win' laka Notoo . . . Boy', a chant which we had learnt from our elders, which chant was supposed to rile Chester no end. He hated the nickname 'Notoo-Boy', and the chant itself made him see red. It was the characteristic bounce with which he walked which had first seemed to suggest to the villagers that he could fly on the wind at any moment. 'Up di win' . . . ' they called out

We tried signalling him from the distance to indicate Chester.

when they saw him. These shouts were supposed to render Chester powerless and to all appearances they did as he would sit calmly on the koker until we stopped and then he would move on. The village story was that he was trying to memorise a voice so that he could know when he caught the right person. Chester had the memory of an elephant, but for days after we had teased him we gave him a wide berth because he was supposed to forget us after a full moon had passed.

Then one day we passed Chester without our normal ringleader. We edged by on the far side of the road and as we moved nearer home we chanted 'Up di win' . . . '

With our backs towards home and our faces towards Chester we kept up our chants. Chester sat with a prophetic calm at the side of the koker. He seemed to sense that his moment of triumph could not have been far away. Then Charles emerged from the school gap closely followed by our teacher Aunt Olive. He was passing close to the koker. We tried signalling him from the distance to indicate Chester, but he smiled and waved back at us. As he got near, Chester pounced on him. He placed Charles's neck lovingly between his paralysed arm and his side and squeezed, gently at first and with gradually increasing pressure. It seemed as though Chester could continue squeezing for an eternity. Charles's feet were kicking frantically in mid-air. Suddenly his body went limp, his legs stopped kicking. Chester continued squeezing with the sadistic delight of long-awaited revenge. His eyes were delirious with glee.

Aunt Olive was now on the scene begging, pleading and threatening. All to no avail. Chester merrily increased the pressure and as he did so the seams in his clothing began to open. Two men rushed to the scene and prised Chester's arms away. As his arms came away the seams in his clothing came apart. The accident took place, and Chester stood body bare before them.

IAN ROBERTSON

Time for Talking and Writing

1. Select *three* things which you find fascinating about Chester from paragraph one.
2. What rumours did the villagers spread about Chester? How did they get their information about him?
3. Did Chester have friends in this village? Quote *one* detail which can support your view.
4. Why did people think Chester was a man who had returned from the dead?
5. In spite of what the villagers thought about him Chester remained in the village. Can you suggest why he didn't go away?
6. How did the village children feel about Chester? How did they try to provoke him?
7. Why was a particular set of words used by the children when they provoked him?
8. Explain exactly how Chester managed to catch Charles. How was Charles punished by Chester?
9. Who helped to free Charles? What must have held a special interest for the other children after Charles was freed from Chester?
10. Chester was physically ugly and his behaviour was ugly. Refer to specific details which give us these impressions.
11. Why do you think the writer of the story chose that particular title for the story instead of a title like 'Chester'?
12. Look up the meaning of these words: attributed; daubed; atheist; agnostic; delirious.
13. How do you know that the writer seemed to be out of sympathy with Chester and wanted others to share that feeling too?

After the Game

Ever since I can remember, Edwin and I've been friends. Primary School and now College in the same form. Every afternoon after school his mother picked us both up in her car and dropped me off at my home before going to their home a few streets away–until some weeks ago.

The morning of that first day when Edwin's mother stopped picking me up after school, as I was having breakfast, my mother told me that my father would call for me later after school.

'Why, Mom?' I asked.

'We've made some new arrangements.' She seemed uncomfortable, as if the new arrangements had caused some embarrassment.

'O.K., Mom,' I said. 'I'll wait for Dad.' But I had an uneasy feeling that something had gone wrong. I hoped that whatever it was, it would right itself again soon.

At school I told Edwin that his mother wouldn't be picking me up any more, but that my father would be picking me up later.

'Why?' he asked. He didn't know anything about the new arrangements.

'You know what I think, Edwin?'

'What?'

'I think our parents have some sort of quarrel.'

Somehow I felt that for no reason our friendship was being threatened and I was determined to preserve it at all costs; yet, that afternoon as he drove away with his mother, I found myself beginning to hate him against my own inclinations and desperately wanting some reason to justify it. It was as if the house that I lived in, or, more precisely, the house of myself, was being blown away by fringe winds of a hurricane which had struck with its full fury elsewhere. As I stood there still waiting for my father I did find that my friend had looked a bit smug and superior as he drove away.

Mr Kelly, the English master, came up. 'Hey, Steve?'

'Hello, Mr Kelly.'

'I thought I saw Edwin's mother drive away.'

'I think they've got an appointment–or something. I'm waiting for my father.'

Edwin hadn't gone ten minutes and it had begun already. The lying with the straight face as it was too difficult and confusing to tell the truth. If I had said 'Our parents have quarrelled', it would have been too embarrassing. He might have asked 'What about?' and then what would I say? I didn't know, myself. It was better to say they had an appointment or something and I was waiting for my father.

When my father arrived I got into his car without saying a word. When we were about half-way home he turned to me and said 'Steve, you're unusually quiet. Is anything the matter?'

'You tell me,' I said.

He was evidently taken aback by my reply. 'We've had a disagreement, Mr Callender and I,' he said, after a few moments. 'He called me a thief.'

'Called you a thief?' I repeated, surprised. So that was it. 'Why?' I said. Immediately I was on my father's side without wanting to know the reason why Mr Callender had called my father a thief. Knowing why wouldn't have made any difference at all.

Edwin and I sat next to each other in class and I immediately began to worry how we were going to get along from tomorrow onwards. I surely wouldn't be the one to speak first. He had called my father a thief–or at least his folks, which was about the same thing.

The trouble between my father and Mr Callender had begun when my father had sold a five-million dollar industrial policy to a new firm that had set up business in Trinidad. Both my father and Edwin's father were insurance underwriters. My father represented a Canadian company and Mr Callender a local one. Mr Callender had accused my father of black-balling his company. My father had said that it was sheer salesmanship and a bit of luck. But Mr Callender had been very hurt for not having copped the big policy with the big commission that it would have brought him.

The next day Edwin said nothing to me. I had hoped he would have talked to me first. Before the day was over the boys of my class were asking both Edwin and me what had happened between us. 'Did we have a quarrel? Was it a girl?' Neither of us told them anything. Whatever had happened between our families was our own private affair.

Things got neither better nor worse for the next few weeks. We just avoided each other as much as possible. Sometimes I felt utterly stupid and empty; stifled. I longed to reach out to Edwin; to talk to him; to go to the school snackette, both of us, together, as we had always done. He had done me nothing, personally, nor I, him. If we had, I knew we would have patched it up long ago. Yet, here we were because of a quarrel between our parents, stifling the most important thing in our lives. Still, I did not speak to him, go up to him and say 'Edwin, aren't we acting like a couple of fools?' Perhaps he would not be ready for the reconciliation that was not really necessary. Perhaps, deep down, I was afraid. I missed him.

An important fixture, the Junior Secondary Schools' Football Competition, was coming around. When the list of players was posted on the School Notice Board, I saw that we were both in the team.

During the match we often found ourselves, for some strange reason when the ball was between us, rushing, not at the ball but at each other. The result was that the players from the opposing side always got control of the ball. Our school lost the game three goals to one and they put the blame entirely on our shoulders. We knew it was true and both ran away from the field as soon as it was possible. We felt like traitors.

The shortest way to our home from the football field lay through a meadow with a ravine, bridged by the trunk of a great tree, running irregularly across it. The ravine, practically dry at this time of the year, was about eight feet deep. When I was some distance from the bridge I looked back and saw Edwin following. The sun was setting. Why hadn't I seen him before? Had he been hurrying to catch up with me? Or had I been going too slowly in the

We fought fiercely for several minutes.

unconscious hope that he was travelling somewhere behind?

At the beginning of the bridge, a few feet from the edge of the ravine, I stopped and turned. When he came up to me we stood looking at each other. He turned away and tried to get on to the tree trunk. I blocked his way. 'You coward,' I said. I wanted to bring the quintessence of insult into that word.

'It's both of us who lost the match,' he said.

'I know.' But I wasn't thinking about the match. I was thinking that his father had called my father a thief and I believe he knew that's what I was thinking and he was thinking that, too.

Without any further warning I cuffed him in the mouth. He put his left hand to his mouth and felt the blood. He doubled his fist and cuffed me in my mouth. I didn't defend myself. We looked at each other. Then, I reached out to him and grabbed him while he grabbed me in turn and we both fell. We fought fiercely for several minutes.

I vaguely remember falling into the ravine. When my senses fully returned I was lying at the bottom of the ravine and Edwin, with bruises and scratches on his face, was leaning over me. I couldn't move my left arm which was folded under me. It was broken.

'I'm sorry,' he said.

'My arm, Edwin,' I said. 'My arm. I think it's broken.'

He rolled me over and took out my arm. It pained a lot, sending a great wave of agony through my whole body and I cried out.

'I'm sorry,' he said.

'I'm sorry, too, Edwin,' I said. 'Tell me, Edwin, what was it all about?'

'I don't know, Steve. You tell me. You started it.'

I tried to move my arm but only grunted with pain.

'I'll go and see if I can get some help,' he said.

He returned with his father but I had already been taken out of the ravine by some other persons coming from the match, short-cutting through the meadow.

I was taken to hospital where I remained for two days, during which time Edwin's parents and my parents visited me. I watched them beside my bed talking to one another as if nothing had happened. The fight between Edwin and me had purged the blind abcess of our hatred and we knew that we had fought because we were compelled to, to break down the wall that our elders were consolidating between us.

Edwin and I were back in class together after a week exactly as before, except that my arm was in plaster, but we shared the satisfaction, of which neither of us spoke with any directness, of having brought our parents together.

BARNABAS J. RAMON-FORTUNÉ

Time for Talking and Writing

1. Why did Edwin's mother stop picking up Steve after school? Who told Steve the reason for the new arrangements?
2. Why do you think Steve's mother avoided giving him a definite reason for the change? Was this a sensible way to handle the situation?
3. What instant effect did the new arrangement seem to be having on Edwin and Steve?
4. Why did Steve invent an untrue reason for not going home with Edwin when Mr Kelly asked?
5. Explain fully what Steve learned was the real reason for the uncomfortable situation between his family and the Callenders.
6. What *three* things must Steve and Edwin have enjoyed a lot together?
7. Did the other boys in the class observe any change between Steve and Edwin? What reason did they suggest for the change?
8. How did Edwin and Steve carry over their new attitude to each other on the football field? What was the effect of that on the outcome of the football match?
9. At what time did that football match end? Pick out a single sentence which tells the time clearly.

10. Who started the quarrel on the way home after the match, Edwin or Steve? Who hit whom first? What was the end of that fight?

11. Though Edwin and Steve fought each other savagely, they became peacemakers. Explain how this was so.

12. Can you suggest, from reading the story, what the writer of the story feels about some adults and their attitude to each other?

13. What qualities do younger children seem to have that adults seem to lack? Why was it easier for the boys to bring about a reunion of the families than for the adults themselves to do it?

14. Pick out the *true* and *false* statements and say why they are true or false.
    (i) The house Steve lived in was blown away by fringe winds of a hurricane.
    (ii) Edwin's father, Mr Callender, thought Steve's father was a dishonest man.
    (iii) Steve wasn't really bothered too much that he and Edwin were no longer close friends.
    (iv) Edwin and Steve had a big fight on the football field and that was what landed Steve in the hospital.

15. Find out the meanings of the following words and phrases: an insurance underwriter; not having copped the big policy; black-balling; reconciliation; quintessence.

Ramgoat Salvation

Thursday evening in Port-of-Spain, and the boys liming in their usual spot.

'Man, I too fed up with this life, nah, same thing every day,' remarked Jackie, the tallest and most aggressive of the group.

There were grunts of agreement all around.

'This city life killing. Wha' we need is a holiday,' continued Jackie.

Pete, always on the outskirts of the group, but always anxious to prove his worth, said, 'I have family live in the country, Jackie. They gone spend ah week in Tobago. How 'bout we go spend ah weekend in they house?'

There was enthusiastic response from the boys, but Jackie, not wishing to appear too impressed, asked, 'Where this house, boy?'

'Quite Rio Claro, man; is real bush, buh is a good change.' Pete, basking in the limelight, was eager to please the powerful Jackie.

Jackie, having established who was boss, shrugged his shoulders.

'O.K.,' he commented, 'then if all yuh feel is good idea, we go leave tomorrow. Five o'clock sharp we meeting here; sharp, no Trinidad time stupidness. That place Rio Claro aint play is joke to get to, yuh know.'

On Friday evening the boys all turned up on schedule and began the long trek to the outback, as they considered it. Nearly three hours later, they piled out of the taxi, and began to walk along the lonely unlit country road.

'Oh Gawd, boy,' exclaimed one of the group, 'yuh mean they aint have street lights self! Is bush country in trute.'

The six of them walked very close together, eyeing the bushes on either side of the road, evidently expecting dire happenings.

Jackie, trying to keep his cool, interjected, 'Buh all yuh too coward! Pete, how far this house now?'

'We almost there, Jackie.'

Then, seemingly right in the middle of nowhere, the house loomed before them.

'Yuh have the key, boy, for Gawd's sake, open the door.'

Pete produced the key, but finding the keyhole was another matter. 'Strike a match, all yuh, I carn't see ah thing.'

Finally the door was opened, and the six of them attempted to get through the doorway together.

'Wait nah, buh wha' happen to all yuh?' Jackie tried to assert his authority. 'Switch on the light and leh we have some grog.'

Pete rejoined timidly, 'They aint have lights quite out here, Jackie, is only lamp and thing.'

Jackie expostulated, 'Buh wha' the france this is at all? Is wild west we in or wha'?'

Then the boys, lighting matches, groped around for a lamp.

There were sounds of a crash. 'Oh Lord, me toe break!'

Then came a cry of triumph. 'I fine it, man, I fine it.'

'Well, wha' yuh waiting for? Light the so-and-so thing, nah.'

'How the hell I go light it?' was the retort. 'I aint never seen ah ting like this in all me born days.'

Jackie moved towards the boys, the heavy responsibility of leadership in his voice.

'Gawd, all yuh carn't do one thing for yuhselves!'

He took the matches. Soon, however, exasperated he remarked, 'Buh this kinda lamp must be invented in the dark ages, fuh trute. How yuh supposed to light the so-and-so thing?'

Pete, eager to regain his popularity, pushed forward.

'I can light it, Jackie.'

With the lamp lit, the boys reorganised themselves. The room glowed warmly. It was comfortably furnished.

'This place aint bad at all, boy,' Jackie condescended to inform the grateful Pete. 'Where the rum? Leh we have ah drink.'

Cosily seated, the boys passed the bottle from one to the

other until each had had a good swig. Their spirits rose, and the boys, wanting to show how unaffected they were by the dark country night outside, began to relate Nancy stories.

Now let us leave the boys for a while, and pay a visit to the house, or to be more specific, the yard of one Ramjohn, about a mile from the house in which the boys were settled.

This Ramjohn was the proud possessor of a ram goat, renowned for miles for his ferocious appearance. In fact, it was the proud boast of the villagers that if you searched the whole of Trinidad and Tobago you could not find his equal.

On this particular night on which our story takes place, Ramgoat, as was his wont, began his leisurely stroll around his domain. Big, white and whiskered he strolled, master of all he surveyed. His territory encompassed an area of some three miles and, needless to say, included the house of Pete's relatives.

Meanwhile, back at the house, the story-telling was proceeding apace. The boys, to prove their city sophistication, laughingly exchanged tales of jumbies and soucouyants. Then Jackie interrupted the proceedings.

'Where the toilet, Pete?'

Pete was once again on a sticky wicket.

'They aint have one inside the house, Jackie, but the latrine just outside.'

Country life by this time held few surprises for Jackie. 'Is O.K., boy, I go fine it.'

Jackie plunged into the black country night, and in so doing displayed a courage equal to that of a latter-day Spartacus.

The faint outline of the latrine could dimly be seen a little distance away.

'I aint able with that at all,' Jackie muttered, and headed for some bushes more conveniently situated. As he approached the chosen area, the bushes began to move.

'Must be a dog!'

Then the bushes parted, and looking at the panic-stricken Jackie was the ugliest red-eyed monster this side of Hades.

For an instant Jackie was glued to the spot. Then the need for self-preservation asserted itself, and he took to flight.

No sound as yet emerged from his paralysed throat as he beat his retreat, but when he burst into the house, speech returned with a vengeance.

'Oh Gawd, Oh Gawd, I see a jumbie.'

Trembling all over, Jackie dropped to the floor. There was consternation all around as the boys listened to his account of the creature in the bushes.

'It had horns, man, about ten feet long, and fire was pouring out of its mouth.'

The story of the encounter, like most tales, gained a lot in the narration. The boys were petrified. This was their fearless leader–the terror of Belmont–speaking!

'Is the devil hisself yuh done see!'

All eyes turned accusingly to Pete. 'Yuh aint tell us this place haunted!'

Defensively, Pete mumbled, 'Buh I aint know, I aint know.'

The six of them sat huddled around the lamp. 'Oh Gawd, as soon as day break, we getting out ah here.'

Outside in the bushes Ramgoat was quite delighted with this break in his routine. The effect he had had on Jackie was gratifying. The villagers rarely responded to even his most ill-tempered charge with such spectacular display.

Intrigued, Ram moved towards the house to investigate these promising newcomers. A few quick butts at the door produced little satisfaction–for Ram that is!

Inside the house the effect was nerve-shattering. The boys shook and prayed. 'Oh lorse, oh lorse, we go dead tonight.'

Ram continued his tour of inspection and reached a window. He looked in. Smokey, sitting frozen at the end of a bed–for by now the boys had retired three to a bed–was the first to see the apparition at the window.

In a second he dived into the bed, landing heavily between his two partners. The two victims of this onslaught reacted violently.

'Wha' happen? Wha' happen?'

Speechlessly, Smokey pointed at the window, and all eyes turned in that direction. The white face of Ramgoat filled the window, and Ram, feeling good-tempered, gave what he considered a friendly grin.

The boys saw the yellow teeth; the eyes in the reflection

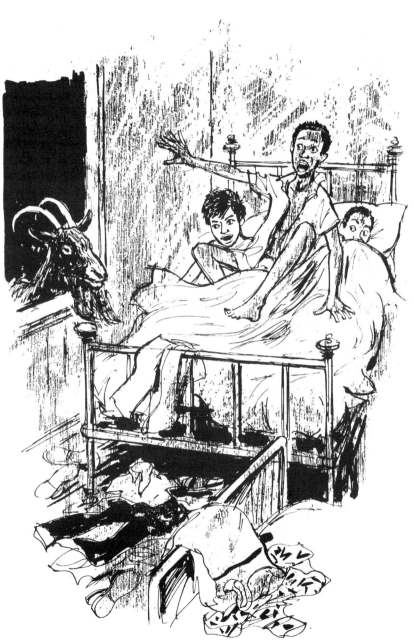

Speechlessly, Smokey pointed at the window.

of the lamp glowed redly. The night and the boys' imagination did the rest. Now from way down in their subconscious, long forgotten prayers emerged. Jackie began the Rosary, Smokey shouted 'Make the sign of the cross, for Gawd's sake, all yuh.' Vishnu, the only Hindu among them, began to chant loudly in Hindustani.

Outside the house, Ramgoat became tired of the whole thing and headed for home. Way up in the heavens, the Recording Angel in charge of prayer finally traced the names of the six. His tardiness in doing this was not in any way a reflection on his efficiency, but rather on the rarity of communication from that source.

Six months later, the scene is once again a Port-of-Spain street. A crowd has gathered, and in the middle of the crowd stands a tall figure in white, addressing the assembly in fiery tones.

'Repent, I say repent, for the day of judgement is at hand. Right now Lucifer walks the earth to claim his own.'

Loud 'Amens' filled the air around.

A woman in the crowd turned to her neighbour. 'Buh this preacher great, yuh hear! He and his five disciples they does go all about the country converting people, and at one time, yuh know, gurl, he was one badjohn!'

'How he get so then?' her neighbour inquired.

'That is ah next thing, gurl! He and the boys spend a night in the country an' they catch the spirit.'

The two women nodded sagely.

'Is so it does happen, gurl,' said one. 'Salvation does come in strange ways.'

IDA RAMESAR

Time for Talking and Writing

1. How many limers sat talking about their boredom on

that Thursday evening? Who emerged as their leader? And why was it that person?

2. Why did the limers decide to go into the country for a while? What aided their plan?

3. There is a word in paragraph two which describes the character of the limers in Port-of-Spain. Write down that word. Then next to it write another word which has the same meaning.

4. How did the limers behave as they reached the country? Are they somewhat changed?

5. The holiday mood started right away on the first night they were in the country. How did they begin this enjoyment?

6. Why did Jackie go outside the house? What did he see and how did he react to that? What effect had that on the other boys?

7. Ramgoat enjoyed welcoming the limers. How did Ramgoat do that?

8. The influence of Ramgoat on the townboys was stunning. What did they think Ramgoat was and how were they changed?

9. We get a new picture of the town limers at the end of the story. How are they different from when we met them at the start of the story? Are you impressed?

10. Is the end of the story one you laugh at, or are you moved to pity? Give reasons for your impressions.

11. Is the writer of this story condemning the limers, laughing at them, or trying to emphasise their better nature? Why do you say so?

12. Put into your own words what you think these words and phrases mean: Trinidad time; latrine; panic-stricken; the need for self-preservation asserted itself; tardiness; badjohn.

Tantie Gertrude

The trouble really started the Sunday evening when Tantie Gertrude spotted Annetta walking home with Paulton. Annetta hadn't realised that her Tantie had seen her. She had taken this chance because she was so sure that Tantie was at evensong. Even so, just to be on the safe side, she had asked Paulton to turn back just before they reached Central Street. But Tantie had missed evensong that night. There had been a meeting of the Mothers' Union and afterwards, she and Daisy and Merle had done some sick-visiting. They had stopped in at old Ma Stevens and the old lady had been so glad to be able to transfer her chatter from her bedpost to real live people that when finally they got away, it was long past evensong time. So, Tantie Gertrude had spotted Annetta just as Paulton furtively grabbed her hand and squeezed it.

Tantie stormed into the little sitting-room, her bosom heaving. Dalma, Annetta's brother, was sprawled in the yellow armchair, his feet up in the pink one. A record spun on the portable record player, and the Mighty Sparrow recounted in song the troubles of a cuckold.

'Annetta! Annetta!' bawled Tantie, 'just come out here this minute.' Annetta appeared hesitantly from her room, her face a picture of apprehension.

'You good-for-nothing young girl,' Tantie stormed. 'You think I didn't see you, eh! Meeting men in the road! You have no shame, girl? After all the trouble I take to train the two of you in a decent God-fearing way! After the example I myself set you . . . I tired warn you. Your mother was a bad woman. She wouldn't listen to people . . . Always saying how your father was going to marry her, till he disappeared, God only knows where. So, you miss, when you find yourself in trouble, don't cross this door-mouth at all, you hear?'

Tantie stormed into the little sitting roon.

'But Tantie . . .,' Annetta pleaded in a contrite voice.

'Don't "Tantie" me, girl! This walking about in the street with a young man will bring you no good, you hear? One thing leads to another. You better listen to what I am telling you. I have more experience than you.'

Dalma sucked his teeth. 'Oh, and how you get it? I thought you always say how you never in your life have anything to do with men and how you devote your whole life to the church.'

Tantie was, by this time, visibly shaking with anger. She turned from Annetta to Dalma.

'The rudeness of this boy! What I do to deserve this? I work myself to the bone for somebody else's children and all I get is rudeness and sorrow. Just look at you! This good Sunday evening, instead of being in church, praising the Lord that you have a roof over your head and food to eat, you cock up in the place listening to those vulgar calypsoes. I don't know why you don't go and find some work. Eighteen years old and all day you idle round town and in the evening you find nothing better to do but listen to those dirty calypsoes, or end up in Black Power meetings. And that's another thing I want to talk to you about. Dalma! I'm talking to you! Where you going, Dalma? I'm speaking to you, boy. Come back here . . .'

But Dalma was already in the road. Annetta could stop and listen to Tantie Gertrude if she cared, but he had had enough.

Dalma knew he had been rude. He tried hard not to be, but Tantie Gertrude seemed to be getting under his skin more and more often these days, especially since he had failed his 'A' Levels. He always felt a twinge of conscience after these outbursts because, despite her infuriating straitlaced attitudes and narrow views, Tantie had been good to them.

Dalma sometimes wondered vaguely about his hazy origins in the small island from which Tantie Gertrude had brought them when, as she told them, their mother died leaving him only two months old and Annetta just a year, but he never gave it much thought for Tantie Gertrude had been mother and father to them. At her age she still worked long hours on her feet before coming home to do the chores. His awareness of how hard she worked made her accusations of his laziness all the more painful.

It was not that he didn't want work, but how could he condemn himself to a stultifying life behind a desk in a stuffy, paper-bound office? He wanted to be outside, to use his hands, to actually see the results of his labours. For a long time he despaired of getting a job and when he had made a half-hearted application for clerical work, it seemed that every youth in the island was applying for the same job – and all complete with 'A' Levels at that!

But now it looked as if he would get exactly what he wanted. He had met Johnnie at a meeting of the Afro-Caribbean Movement. Johnnie had just returned to the West Indies after eighteen years in England and he was able to offer first-hand accounts of the problems of a black man in a hostile white society. Now he was back home, a qualified motor engineer with new tools, new ideas, the latest equipment and techniques. Dalma found himself drawn to him and, in their discussions after, Johnnie had mentioned his new car-repair garage.

Dalma showed immense interest and Johnnie was very quick to invite him along to learn the trade.

'You remind me of myself when I was younger,' Johnnie had said. 'I wanted to use my hands, but no one around me seemed to understand. I left the little island where I grew up, just to get away from the *respectable* white-collar job I was expected to live – and die at.'

Johnnie had seemed pensive for a while.

'I'll pay you, of course, Dalma,' he had continued, 'if you want the job. There's a really good future in this business if you're good at it.' Naturally, Dalma had accepted with alacrity.

He quickened his pace now as he realised that he was late for his meeting with Johnnie at the garage.

'Thought you weren't going to make it, mate,' said Johnnie in that strange-sounding accent of his. Dalma still found that the English accent jarred. The English accent didn't fit a black face. He shrugged.

'Oh, another set of fussing at home, you know. I've told you what Tantie is like.'

'Yes,' murmured Johnnie thoughtfully. 'P'raps I'd better go along and talk to your Auntie Gertrude, seeing that I'll soon be your employer.' He grinned. 'She'll probably want to be sure I'm of sound character.'

Dalma smiled uncertainly. 'Oh, I don't know if that's necessary.' He wasn't exactly keen to introduce Johnnie at a moment of domestic strife.

'Come on,' said Johnnie decisively. 'I want to see your Tantie Gertrude.' He smiled strangely. Dalma gave him a puzzled look, shrugged, and they set off for home.

You could hear Tantie Gertrude from the front gate. Once she got started, it was the devil's own work to stop her.

'. . . and when I was your age, they didn't have any of this girlfriend boyfriend nonsense. If you were a decent girl, you would find yourself behind your front door long before dark instead of . . . '

'Tantie Gertrude!' Dalma tried to stem the flow. 'Somebody out here to see you.'

'Who? I'm not expecting anybody. Merle?' Tantie Gertrude came out of the kitchen, wiping her hands on the dishcloth.

'Good afternoon, Gertrude,' said Johnnie softly. Tantie stopped short. She stood stock still and slowly the dishcloth dropped, her jaw dropped, and she sank into the pink armchair.

'Johnnie,' she croaked.

Dalma goggled. 'You know him?'

'Yes, she knows me, Dalma,' said Johnnie in his English accent. 'Of course she knows your father.'

Silence.

'Is true, Tantie Gertrude?'

Before she could answer, Johnnie interposed. 'Not "Tantie Gertrude"', he said. '"Mummy"!'

OLIVER FLAX

Time for Talking and Writing

1. On what evening of the week did Annetta and Paulton walk home together? Why did they choose that particular evening for their outing?
2. What was the relationship between Annetta and Paulton? Quote one detail from paragraph one which helps to emphasise their relationship.
3. How did Tantie behave after she saw the goodbye of Annetta and Paulton that evening? Should Tantie have settled the matter differently?
4. What reason did Tantie give for taking so stern an attitude to Annetta's relationship with Paulton?
5. Whose side did Dalma take in the quarrel between Tantie and Annetta?
6. What helped to turn Dalma into such a rude boy? Did he really dislike Tantie? Refer directly to any detail from the story which will support your view.
7. Who and what helped to relieve Dalma of his boredom?
8. Why was Johnnie able to understand Dalma so quickly and so easily?
9. Why was Johnnie about to visit Tantie?
10. Quite a surprise meets us at the end of the story. Can you work out for yourselves the connections among the four persons, Tantie, Annetta, Johnnie and Dalma?
11. Before we get to the end of the story, there is a little hint of some connection between Johnnie and Dalma. Find out where that hint is.
12. Why do you think Tantie felt she should keep the facts from Annetta and Dalma about their parents? Why in the circumstance was Tantie right in doing so? Why was she at fault?
13. In the light of what was revealed at the end of the story how do you think Tantie would now behave towards Annetta and Paulton?

The Cousins

What is nicer, when you are an only child, than hearing that some cousins are coming to live at your home? Celia was so excited that she could hardly eat on the day that they were expected to arrive. She jibbered and jabbered all day, nearly driving her mother insane, and spent most of her time at the gate looking out for Uncle Jed's car. Celia's mother was not too sure that she shared the child's excitement. Those boys, coming from the country and belonging to a large family, were used to doing whatever they liked – and often what they liked was pure mischief. Celia's mother considered them to be very badly brought up and privately criticised her sister for being such an indulgent mother. Anyway, for better or worse, they were coming to town to go to high school and would have to live with the Wilsons during the school term.

A blue Vauxhall suddenly appeared at the end of the road and threw Celia into ecstasies of glee. 'They coming, they coming, they coming, they coming . . .' Round and round the words danced with Celia towards the gate. Soon, Ronald and James – or Dingo and Jiggs, as they were called within the family – jumped out of the car, wide grins on their sunburnt faces. There was a grand hugging-up, lots of joking and teasing. Dingo, tall and very dark, was a year older than Celia; Jiggs, lean and brown, a few months younger. They were perfect playmates for each other. As the boys moved boisterously towards the room which would be theirs to put down their luggage, it seemed to Celia's mother that the whole house trembled and shook. She took a last quick look at the orderly arrangement of her living room, the virgin purity of her white drapes and quietly said 'goodbye' to it all.

'Yes, Lord, it has started already,' Celia's mother said to herself as she moved quickly towards the sound. Dingo stood in one corner of the boys' room, looking extremely foolish. Jiggs, sitting on one of the beds, was grinning at his brother's discomfiture. On the floor near Dingo's right foot lay the remains of a bedside lamp. Mrs Wilson thanked her stars that she had had the good sense to put in the boys' room an old lamp that she had never liked. Fixing her face firmly, however, she enquired into the circumstances of the accident. Trying to look remorseful, Dingo explained that he had 'only' been moving the lamp into the corner when it slipped from his hand.

'Why didn't you leave it where it was, between the two beds?' his aunt asked.

No reply.

Celia was standing in the doorway looking on anxiously. Her mother could not bear to spoil this first day.

'All right, pick up the pieces and put them in the garbage can,' she said, and walked out.

That night, instead of staying indoors and reading by herself, Celia played in the garden with the boys and two children from next door. What fun! She was excited by the fresh, fragile smells of the night, the coolness of the air on her skin, the unaccustomed quiet of the street. Inside the house, Mrs Wilson heard Celia's high-pitched laughter and could feel the excitement running like a thread through the young voice. Maybe having Dingo and Jiggs was not too high a price to pay for making Celia so happy, she thought.

The children had decided on a game of hide-and-seek. Celia was 'it'. After giving them time to hide, she set off happily to find them. She soon found Jean and Bobby, the next-door children, crouching behind a coconut tree, but nowhere could she find Dingo and Jiggs. After a long while, Jean and Bobby started to help her search, but they had no better success. Eventually, Celia–not too pleased–had to shout out:

'I give up! Dingo and Jiggs, I give up!'

Two minutes later, they were at her side, laughing in triumph.

'But where were you?' she asked, puzzled. She was so sure that she knew her own yard better than anyone else. They would not tell her.

The children had decided on a game of hide-and-seek.

'My turn now,' said Bobby, and the others ran to hide as he started to count. Celia was hunting for a good hiding-place among the trees near to the fence when she heard a low hiss. She looked around keenly, but though her eyes were used to the darkness, she could see no one. The hiss came again–surely from very near? Celia turned this way and that, trying to see with her whole body, to pierce the darkness. As the sound came again, she rushed straight towards it and then gasped in surprise as she felt flesh against her face and outstretched hands.

'Quiet!' a voice buzzed low in her ear as a hand gripped her arm to steady her. Then she realised what the scamps had been doing. Dingo and Jiggs had taken off their shirts. In the moonless dark of the night, their brown skins would make them invisible. Their pants, being a dull khaki, were quite safe from detection. She wanted to laugh out, but Bobby would be sure to hear. In fact, he was already coming in their direction. Celia was hastily pushed behind Jiggs and cautioned to stay absolutely still. As Bobby approached, it gave her a strange feeling to know that he was looking straight at them and could not see them. She felt as though she really was invisible, as if she needed his seeing her to make her really exist. She felt light, insubstantial, a ghost. Bobby came to within a few feet of them, then wandered off, still searching earnestly.

'Come,' said Jiggs very softly and led her soundlessly away.

'Where you going?' she whispered.

'New hiding-place,' he whispered back and led her to an area which Bobby had already examined. And so it went on, no one able to find Dingo and Jiggs and having to give up in despair or annoyance. Until it was Celia's turn again. She had been quietly thinking of a way to outsmart those boys. She would wipe those grins off their faces. When it was time for her to find the others, she made fierce little rushes into the darkness with her arms held straight out. Sure enough, she soon collided with Dingo. Tricky and slippery as an eel, he tried to wriggle away from her grasp and escape, but she had been expecting this and held on tightly.

'I got Dingo, I got Dingo!' she shouted exultantly.

'No! True?' Jean and Bobby were so excited that they rushed forward to see if it could really be true.

'So that is why we couldn't find you!' Jean exclaimed as they dragged the reluctant Dingo to the verandah steps and saw for the first time that he was shirtless.

'All right,' she raised her voice. 'We know the game now, Mr Jiggs. We coming for you!'

And Celia, Jean and Bobby went forward together to run him to earth. Dingo sat down on a step to watch them. Jiggs, alerted, put out his best efforts to remain free and nearly made it. For a long time the others combed the yard determinedly and kept missing him–just barely missing him. Then Jean tripped and fell quite close to him and Jiggs, the irrepressible joker, could not help snickering. The jig was up. They dragged him in triumph back to the verandah, all laughing immoderately.

'You scamp, you!' Jean slapped him weakly, still doubled up with laughter. 'You scamp, you!'

And so the time passed. Days of school-work and afternoons of play. Mrs Wilson had great trouble getting the children to settle down to serious homework in the evenings. Dingo and Jiggs hated any form of regimentation and could not see why they should do more work at home than they did at school. This, of course, made Celia reluctant to do her work too. One day matters came to a head.

Mr Wilson had come home early for a change because he was not feeling well. He ate very little supper and only sat in the living room because he knew that his wife cherished the opportunity of a little chat with him. Secretly he was pining for his bed–there was nothing so nice, he thought, as a new Science fiction magazine to read before falling asleep. And he had brought one home with him. Still, his wife had looked so pleased to see him home early.
. . . They were sitting there comfortably, easy in each other's presence, the children doing work at the dining-table while the adults talked.

'Hell, I fed up with this Algebra!' Jiggs pushed away the offending and incomprehensible textbook. He sucked his teeth in annoyance. 'What a man have to do all this nonsense for?'

Dingo grinned as usual. He did not understand algebra

any better than his brother but was more imperturbable.

'You want help?' he asked with sweet sarcasm.

'You don't understand it a piece better!' Jiggs frowned, then the quick grin came. 'Let us mash up this homework thing!' he suggested.

'How, boy?' Dingo was always ready for destruction.

Jiggs did not answer. He got up from the table and went outside, soon to return with a piece of wire. He grinned at the other two and waved it significantly. Then he started to unscrew the electric bulb from its socket, holding it with a very dirty handkerchief.

'What you doing?' asked Celia nervously. She loved her cousins but had become apprehensive of the kinds of things they were fond of doing. Still Jiggs grinned, said nothing and persisted. He put the bulb carefully on the table, then wrapped one end of the wire with the handkerchief, held it and started to poke it into the empty socket.

Celia's mother was in the middle of what she thought of as a nice piece of gossip and her husband was longing more and more for his bed when the house suddenly went dark.

'What on earth?' she wondered. 'Don't tell me they cut off the lights again?'

'Must be a fuse,' said her husband, getting up to find the flashlight.

'But the whole house is dark,' she pointed out.

As they went towards the fuse box with the flashlight, she noticed the silence of the children. Something funny, she thought. Sure enough, all the fuses were blown, but the box of spare fuses could not be found.

'We must have finished them,' Mrs Wilson suggested.

'Nonsense, man, I bought a whole new box just the other day.' One could hear the tiredness and annoyance in Mr Wilson's voice. They hunted high and low.

'You children come and help us look for the fuses,' Mrs Wilson urged. They bustled noisily about but she had the distinct feeling that they were not really looking. In fact, more than once she thought she heard a muffled snicker. These children are up to something, she thought and swung her flashlight up to see their faces just in time to catch a wide grin on Jiggs's face. In a second she pounced, grabbing a handful of his shirt as she caught him by the shoulder. 'All right, joker-boy,' she said, anger making her voice low yet resonant. 'Where are those fuses?'

'Ah don't know, Aunty,' Jiggs tried to escape but the strength of her anger held him. 'Ah really don't know. Ah don't know anything about the fuses. True, Aunty . . .'

Suddenly he could not speak at all because she was shaking him, shaking him with a fury that unsettled even his tough little heart.

'Aunty–Aunty,' he gasped finally. 'Aunty, stop–ah–ah threw them outside!'

'You little wretch!' The flashlight fell unnoticed as she used the hand that had held it to slap him hard in the face. 'You disgusting little wretch!' Slap! Slap! 'If I don't find them, I'm going to break your neck.' Slap!

Of course, they could not find the fuses in the dark, even with the help of flashlights. Jiggs had given the throw all the weight of his strong young body. They trooped back inside in a tense silence. Mrs Wilson found some candles and lit them. At any other time, Celia would have loved the candle-light and the softness with which it touched all shapes and faces, but not tonight. She looked at the faces around the table and her mouth trembled involuntarily. Dingo and Jiggs looked scared–she had seen that before. Mama looked murderous–she had seen that before too. But Papa, her quiet, indulgent Papa who was wont to hold her in his arms, always smelling of cologne–she saw Papa as she had never seen him before. The realisation that the boys had deliberately blown the fuses for some obscure reason of their own and callously inconvenienced the whole household, shook him with a rare anger. Normally very considerate himself, he could neither understand nor tolerate such actions.

He raised his arm and for the first time Celia noticed how large it was. So many, many times had she lain in that arm and looked out at the world, feeling secure, utterly content, rocked and babied by the big, gentle man. Now she trembled as if she felt the weight and terror of that ominous upraised arm. Her father was suddenly a stranger. He took a step forward and she cringed away, speechless in fear, but he did not see her–he saw no one but Jiggs, and

Jiggs, pale beneath the brown skin, saw no one but him.

Then like an axe the blow descended. Like a dead log, Jiggs fell to the ground, his neck and shoulder searing with pain. Still fear was stronger and Jiggs half-raised himself on one arm, holding the other protectively over his face. Above him the huge form stood in silent threat while the air trembled around them with unspoken rage. Aside from the involuntary cry of pain that Jiggs had emitted as he fell, there was no sound. The room was absolutely quiet, utterly still.

Then–it seemed like hours–Papa sighed heavily, his arms relaxed and he turned away. He walked to the door, then paused and turned back. He pulled out a chair and sat down.

'You boys come here.' The voice was very still. They obeyed instantly. 'Let me tell you something.' They all listened. 'Your Aunty and I have had just about enough, just–about–enough! You understand?' They nodded, terrified. 'Since you came you been leading your Aunty a dance. You see she is a big woman? Eh? You see?' Dingo and Jiggs nodded quickly. 'Yes, she is a big woman and in her own house. And let me tell you something.' He rose slowly, impelled by the words. Dingo and Jiggs stepped backwards, fear growing in their faces. 'Let me tell you something,' the voice rose too, 'you going to stop this damn stupidness or I'm going to knock you clear back to your mother's house!' The thunder of his voice seemed to shake the room. Celia trembled uncontrollably. Nobody doubted that he could do it. 'You understand?' They nodded dumbly. 'You sure you understand?' Yes, yes, their eager nods seemed to say, we'll do anything, anything. 'All right, get away now.' He waved a huge arm in disgust and Jiggs flinched. 'Get away–go to your bed. Get away from m'sight.' They tripped over each other in their haste to leave the room.

Papa sat back in his chair and looked for the first time at his wife. Slowly he shook his head and raised his eyebrows–it was his way of dismissing an unpleasant matter. She nodded in shared understanding. Then he smiled wryly.

'Father Devil and Mr Satan,' he said, 'and we had to get them both!'

It was a few days before the boys recovered their normal good spirits, but it was weeks before they dared to approach their uncle for even the smallest thing. The transformation of that silent, kindly soul into the awesome thing that had terrified them that night remained forever imprinted on their memories. For Celia it went much deeper than mere fright. She had seen her beloved Papa in a new perspective. She could never snuggle in his arms again without being aware of the terrible force that lay in them. And Papa, rubbing her head fondly and calling her by all the silly names that he had invented just for her, could sense the child's feelings. He could almost hear the silent probing and questioning that went on within her. And to himself he sighed sadly and with some vexation. Those dratted boys! He had yet to meet two children that were more badly brought up than they. And those provoking grins on their faces! He prayed for the holidays to come quickly. He planned to ship them home on the very first day.

Mrs Wilson's thoughts were calmer but she, too, worried about the influence that the boys could have on Celia. She had already grown much louder and more boisterous. One day, Mrs Wilson was scandalised at overhearing Celia tell a neighbouring child:

'Come if you bad! I'll break your tail for you!' And, looking through the window at the warlike gestures and fierce looks with which Celia was threatening the child, she could only stand in amazement. Soon, a rip-roaring battle was in progress; the mother just turned away.

An innocent bicycle, whose owner remains anonymous to this day, brought on the final act of the drama. Indulgent as the boys' parents were, they had never given them bicycles, probably because the farm on which they lived was in a very hilly area. Unaccustomed to being thwarted in anything, Dingo and Jiggs had developed an inordinate passion for bicycles. Whenever they got a chance, they would beg a friend to teach them to ride. One day Mrs Wilson was in the kitchen making a salad to go with the lunch when a loud commotion broke in on her.

'Mama, Mama!' It was Celia, wide-eyed and frightened, with Jiggs and two or three other children close behind. 'Mama, come quick, Dingo–Dingo dead!'

'What?' Her mother wheeled around, dropping lettuce and cucumber slices.

'Yes–come quick! Come, Mama! Come now!'

'Where–what happened?' asked the mother, bending to retrieve the vegetables and mechanically washing them off without even realising it.

'Mama, you have to come now, now, now!'

Impelled by the child's insistence, Mrs Wilson wiped her hands and followed them. She had to trot to keep up with them. Down the road they went, around the corner and up the busy main street (where she had more than once told them not to go). Not far along the road stood Chin's Grocery, a building which, though it had newly been painted in a hopeful blue with touches of yellow, could not hide its run-down condition. Outside of Chin's a small crowd had gathered, talking and pointing excitedly. Mrs Wilson felt instinctively that Dingo was in the centre of that crowd, the object of all the excitement.

They soon reached the crowd and the children elbowed their way importantly to the centre. At first, Mrs Wilson thought her eyes were playing tricks on her. She looked and looked again. Yes, it was Dingo–though it was not easy to recognise that distorted face, twisted with pain and fright. He and a bicycle lay on the ground in so intimate a tangle that it seemed as if they had grown together and were really a single body. The strange twists of his right leg, in particular, told her at once that it was broken, probably in several places. Dear Lord, she thought, dear heavenly Lord! But the inaction of surprise was gone in a minute and she stooped down beside the boy and tried, with the help of some of the men present, to extricate him from the cruel metal.

Poor Dingo screamed and screamed again, despite all their efforts to be as gentle as possible. Finally he was free, but hung like a dead weight in their arms, his right leg flung out from the body and twisted grotesquely. Soon, an ambulance arrived–Mrs Wilson had not even realised that some thoughtful onlooker had gone to call for one – and Dingo, screaming again, was lifted into it. Celia and Jiggs scrambled in after Mrs Wilson, the doors closed and the ambulance drove away, scattering the host of little children who had been clinging to it. At this stage, mercifully, Dingo fainted.

Once Dingo's leg had been set and his various painful bruises attended to, the Wilsons turned their attention to the bicycle and learnt, to their horror, that Dingo had 'borrowed' a bicycle which he had found leaning on a gate. None of the children knew who the real owner was. To make matters worse, Dingo could not even remember exactly where he had found the bicycle. For a long time the Wilsons trembled every time a stranger came to their gate in the fear that he was coming in wrath for his bicycle and some compensation. But no one ever came.

One Sunday morning three weeks later, Celia's Aunt Rosie and Uncle Jed arrived at the Wilsons' house. An incongruous couple they seemed to Celia. Uncle Jed was tall and slim, with thick, wavy hair standing rather like a mane around his head, while Aunt Rosie was short and extremely fat, her short, coarse hair rolled up into little 'China bumps' and stuck with tortoise-shell hairpins that protruded all over her head. Her saving grace was a very interesting face that, when young and slim, must have been compelling in its beauty. Her skin was as dark as her sister's was fair, but one could detect a family resemblance quite easily.

Waiting for them on the verandah were their two very subdued sons. Everyone sat on the verandah for a while, talking rather aimlessly. Mrs Wilson knew that her sister was annoyed with the decision that she had made, though Jed understood. Like it or lump it, she thought fiercely, I don't care.

They soon went inside to have lunch, which was eaten rather silently. Celia looked from face to face, her heart sinking at the thought that this was the last meal that Dingo and Jiggs would be eating as inmates of her home. Was she sad? She did not know. What she did know was that she loved Mama and Papa best, and that both of them had not been themselves since the coming of those boys. She herself had grown wary of following any of their plans because trouble and disaster so often resulted. Yet they had been such fun!

Soon they were making their way to the gate, Dingo

leaning heavily on his crutches and flanked by two anxious parents. A final wave and the blue Vauxhall drove away, bound for the boarding school which was to be the boys' new home during the school term.

'Poor Clairview College!' said Papa with genuine pity in his voice. 'Better they don't know the warm time coming their way!'

JOY MOORE

Time for Talking and Writing

1. Why was Celia so happy that her two cousins were coming to stay at her home? Pick out *three* verbs which show Celia's eagerness.
2. What was the attitude of Celia's mother to the coming of the boys? Why did she feel that way?
3. Who was older, Jiggs or Dingo? In spite of being a girl, why was it easy for Celia to become pals with the boys immediately?
4. Trouble followed the boys as soon as they settled down on the first night. Explain that statement.
5. For Celia a new experience began. What could she do along with the boys that she could not do by herself? How does the writer point out Celia's enjoyment?
6. 'Boys will be boys' goes the saying. How do Dingo and Jiggs trick the others during the hide-and-seek game?
7. Do you think the writer of this story was enjoying the boys' behaviour during the game? Can you say how you detect the writer's feelings?
8. Why didn't Dingo and Jiggs like the idea of homework? Give *two* reasons of your own why you think homework is necessary, and *two* reasons why you think it is a nuisance.

9. When Celia's father enters the story, what impression do you form of him? What helped you to decide on your impressions?

10. Say *briefly* what the boys did on the night they got fed up with their homework.

11. How did Celia feel about this incident? Why didn't she tell her parents on the boys?

12. How did Aunty guess that Jiggs was involved in the lights going out? How did she and Uncle punish Jiggs?

13. Do you think Mr and Mrs Wilson were too severe on Jiggs? Give a reason for your opinion.

14. What final tragedy brought the boys' stay at the Wilsons' to an end? Put your answer into not more than *five* sentences.

15. What kind of influence did the boys have on Celia? What atmosphere did they create at the Wilsons'? Was Celia better off with or without her cousins?

16. i) Why do you think the Wilsons, chiefly Aunty and Uncle, found it hard to put up with the mischief of the boys?

    ii) Think on both sides of the question which follows, and give good reasons for your opinions. Could the Wilsons have been more sympathetic to the boys?

17. What *three* qualities of young school boys did you observe through those two boys, Dingo and Jiggs? Would you call the boys ill-mannered, wicked, brats, happy-go-lucky, or 'great guys'? Give reasons for your answers.

About the Contributors

JOY CLARKE was born in Antigua. She was educated at the Antigua Girls' High School and Waterloo University, Canada. She is married to a Trinidadian, and is a Graduate English Mistress at Queen's Royal College, Trinidad. 'De Trip', which was written specially for this collection, is her first published short story.

OLIVER FLAX was born in Antigua. He was educated at the Antigua Boys' Grammar School and the University of the West Indies, Jamaica. A French Honours Graduate, he taught for a while at Princess Margaret High School, Antigua. He is now Administrative Assistant, West Indies Oil Company, Antigua, and the Editor of the Company Magazine. He has also written a play which has been performed on various occasions by The Little Theatre Group, Antigua. 'Tantie Gertrude', which was written specially for this collection, is his first published short story. He is married and has one son.

BARNABAS J. RAMON-FORTUNÉ, a Trinidadian, has been writing short stories and poetry for a number of years. Several of his poems and some of his short stories first received recognition over the B.B.C. on the programme 'Caribbean Voices'. Up to October 1971, he was employed in the Civil Service, but retired in that year to devote his time to writing. He is married and has twelve children, and much of his work deals with children and their problems, and with parent–children relationships. In recent times, some of his poetry and short stories have been appearing in school textbooks being used in the Caribbean and abroad.

The story 'The Kite', which appears in this collection, was first broadcast over 'Caribbean Voices', and later went on to be acclaimed by the B.B.C. as the most representative West Indian short story broadcast in the entire course of that programme in its coming-of-age edition of 'London Calling'. It has since been published or broadcast no fewer than six times.

NEVILLE GIUSEPPI is a Trinidadian. He retired from the Civil Service in 1969. He is a free-lance writer, poet and essayist, and the author of *A Modern Pilgrim's Scrip* (1938); *The Light of Thought* (1943); *From Grave to Gay* (1959); and *Selected Poems* (1972). His work has also appeared in various anthologies and school textbooks. The B.B.C. gave recognition to some of his poetry on the programme 'Calling the West Indies'. He is married and has a daughter and a son.

UNDINE GIUSEPPI is a Barbadian by birth and a Trinidadian by citizenship. She is the wife of Neville Giuseppi. Formerly Vice-Principal of St. Augustine Girls' High School, Trinidad, for a number of years, she is now the Principal of the University School. Her publications include *These Things are Life*, a collection of short stories and poems, (1944); *Sir Frank Worrell* (1969); *Nelson's New West Indian Readers—Book* 1. (1971); *Nelson's New West Indian Readers—Book* 2 (1971). *Nelson's New West Indian Readers—Book* 4 is due to appear in 1973.

ROBERT PATRICK ST. LEGER HENRY was born in Mandeville, Jamaica. He was educated at Kingston College, the University of the West Indies, and the Institute of Education, London. He was Resident Tutor, Extra-Mural Department of U.W.I., Trinidad, then branched off to the advertising business, only to return to the University as Public Relations Officer. Although he holds a degree in Mathematics and Physics, he has spent his life dabbling in the Arts. He is involved in drama, and he writes – chiefly poems – but his main love is music. His short story 'Give and Take' appeared first in *Focus* (1960).

JOY MOORE was born and grew up in Jamaica. She attended University in Canada, where she met and got married to Eugenio Moore, a Trinidadian. They have two children and live in Trinidad. She is the Head of the English Department at St. Augustine Girls' High School, Trinidad, but she has only recently become interested in writing for publication. 'The Cousins' was written specially for this collection. A shorter version of 'Mama's Theme Song' appeared first in *Writing is Fun,* a collection of short stories and light verse compiled by Undine Giuseppi and published during International Book Year (1972).

IDA RAMESAR is Irish by birth, but she is married to a Trinidadian, and identifies herself with the West Indies. She formerly worked with a Canadian publishing company. She and her husband live in Trinidad, and they have two children. She is now a housewife whose hobby is writing. Her two short stories 'Paradise Lost' and 'Ramgoat Salvation' represent her first published work. They appeared previously in *Writing is Fun,* a collection of short stories and light verse compiled by Undine Giuseppi. 'Paradise Lost' was the prize-winning story in a competition on the Trinidad and Tobago Television programme 'Mainly For Women' in 1972. Mrs Ramesar has since become a regular contributor of articles to the *The Sunday Express,* a local newspaper.

IAN ROBERTSON was born in Georgetown, Guyana. He was educated at Queen's College, Guyana, and the University of the West Indies, Jamaica. He is now a temporary resident in Trinidad, where he is doing Post Graduate work in Linguistics at U.W.I., St. Augustine. 'Up the Wind Laka Notoo-Boy' which was written specially for this collection, is his first published short story.

NINNIE SEEREERAM is an eighteen-year old Trinidadian who has only recently graduated from High School. 'The New Teacher', which appeared previously in *Writing is Fun,* is her first published short story.

FLORA SPENCER is a Barbadian. She is a member of the Governing Body of the Parkinson School, a member of the Executive Committees of both the Barbados Arts Council and the Commonwealth Caribbean Resource Centre. She paints, does a bit of interior decoration, and writes for the press. She has written a television series 'Barbados, Past and Present', and was a script writer for 'Brathwaites of Black Rock', a radio series which was well received in Barbados and in other West Indian islands. She has written short stories for radio, and is a script writer for 'Bimshire', an annual performance first produced for Independence in 1966. Some of her work appears in various West Indian textbooks.

SHIRLEY TAPPIN, a Trinidadian, is a young bank clerk who occasionally writes short stories as a hobby. She is married and has one daughter. Her first effort at writing the short story was 'Backfire' which appears in this anthology. Her inclination towards writing has been fostered by her love of books in a family where reading and writing have held a very high place. She is the daughter of Barnabas J. Ramon-Fortuné. 'Backfire' won the first ever short story competition held on the Trinidad and Tobago Television programme 'Mainly for Women' after a short course on 'The Art of Writing' which was conducted by Mrs Undine Giuseppi in 1971.

C. ARNOLD THOMASOS is a Trinidadian. He is the Speaker of the House of Representatives, Trinidad and Tobago, a post which he has held since 1961. A former teacher and free-lance writer, he is the author of *Poems* (1939), and numerous articles and short stories. His work has appeared in *The Beacon,* and various West Indian anthologies. During the 40's, some of his poems were read on the B.B.C. programme 'Calling the West Indies'. He is married and has five daughters. The short story 'The Teddy Bear' was written specially for this collection.

JOY ACKBARALI, who supplied the sections entitled 'Time for Talking and Writing', is a Trinidadian. She was educated at St. Augustine Girls' High School and at Mt. Allison University, Canada, where she obtained a Bachelor of Arts Degree, with a major in English. She also holds the Bachelor of Education Degree from Dalhousie University. She has been teaching English at secondary level for seven years, six of which have been spent at her Alma Mater, St. Augustine Girls' High School.